T0156668

FROM
Nightmares
to
Sweet Dreams

Letting the Presence of Christ
Transform Our Worst Memories

ജ ൠ

MARK I. PESKE

Order this book online at www.trafford.com
or email orders@trafford.com

Most Trafford titles are also available at major online book retailers.

© Copyright 2013 Mark I. Peske.
All rights reserved. No part of this publication may be reproduced, stored in a
retrieval system, or transmitted, in any form or by any means, electronic, mechanical,
photocopying, recording, or otherwise, without the written prior permission of the author.

Printed in the United States of America.

ISBN: 978-1-4669-9551-2 (sc)
ISBN: 978-1-4669-9550-5 (hc)
ISBN: 978-1-4669-9549-9 (e)

Library of Congress Control Number: 2013908911

Trafford rev. 07/26/2013

www.trafford.com

North America & international
toll-free: 1 888 232 4444 (USA & Canada)
fax: 812 355 4082

Contents

හ ඏ

The book you are now holding contains a very simple message. Let me give it to you in one sentence: *Jesus can transform even our worst memories, leaving us at peace and changing those nightmares into places of sweet communion with him.* He can do it! And that's what this book is all about.

If you've ever gone through bad experiences that left you with painful memories, this message is for you.

If you work as a teacher, counselor, pastor, social worker, or other "people professional," you've probably had people tell you about their experiences of being sexually abused, beaten by a boyfriend or a spouse, mistreated by parents, or exposed to other traumatic experiences. If you've ever wanted to help them overcome the enduring anguish of these memories, this message is for you.

If you are a parent who wants to be equipped to help your child pass through some of the frightening episodes of life without being permanently scarred, this message is for you.

The Indian Style

I work as a missionary to Native American people. In serving Indian people as a messenger of the Good News that Jesus brought, I also learn from them. One of the beautiful aspects of Native American culture is their teaching style. An Indian elder once told me, "Indian people have always used *stories* to teach their moral values and oral history." The more I got used to this approach, the more I liked it. Stories are easy to listen to and easy to remember. Jesus used stories. As a matter of fact, the Gospels say he never taught anything without using stories.

This book is basically a collection of stories—stories of the opportunities I have had helping people look to Jesus for healing from their most traumatic experiences.

Another tenant of teaching in the Indian style is that rather than trying to explain everything exhaustively, it is better to lead a learner to the edge of discovery and then step back, allowing the learner to take the final steps and make the discovery his own.

So in this book, I've tried not to get in the way of your discovery. What I'd like to do is invite you along on some of the adventures that I've had. I want to let you sit beside me and listen as I've conversed with people, watching as we bring painful memories into the light. I want you to observe what happens when we bring these experiences to Jesus in prayer. I want to let you discover Jesus as the Healer of our hearts. And I want to let him teach you what you will need to know to take steps of healing for your own nightmares or those of people you know.

In Chronological Order

When I started, I did not want to write this book. The chief reason was that even after I began praying with people for healing from the emotional wound of the past, I still felt there was so much I *didn't* know. Even when Jesus would answer our prayers and people experienced startling transformations of their traumatic memories, I wondered if I was really doing it right. In my mind, other people were "experts." I was just a struggling young man, feeling my way along as best I could through the dark world of people's problems. I hoped I was helping them connect with Christ in a way that would help them step out of the darkness and into his light, but was I really?

Then it occurred to me that dealing with people's most painful memories is always a delicate and somewhat frightening thing. Anyone who goes there with someone else is going to feel at least a little afraid. (It's probably good that we do! This world is too delicate to go in with a careless or cavalier attitude.) So I decided to arrange the healing stories in this book in a roughly chronological order. I want to let you see my humble beginnings. I hope you can spot my early uncertainties. I hope you can observe how I grew in my own understanding. I hope you can sense how I gained confidence that Jesus really can change our nightmares into sweet dreams. And I hope you will allow yourself the same room to grow that God allowed me.

I know how scary it is to look someone in the eye and say "Would you like to pray with me and ask God to help you with that memory?" And I suspect you will feel the same reluctance to pray with the people in your life, which I also experienced. But ultimately, fear is the tool of the devil to immobilize us and prevent us from serving God as we are led by his Word and Spirit. Don't let the devil get away with whispering in your ear, "You can't do this! Other people are experts, but you don't know what you're doing. You'll probably do more harm than good!"

Jesus wants to bring peace to your most traumatic memories. And he wants us to help one another bring our burdens to him so that he can set us free from the chains of the past. He will help us even when our faith is small. And remember—only by exercise will our faith grow.

How It Began for Me

In 1998, I began working at a drug and alcohol treatment center one day a week. My job was to listen to people's fifth step. This step in the twelve steps of Alcoholics Anonymous says,

"We admitted to God, ourselves, and another human being, the exact nature of our wrongs." It gives people a chance to tell their life story, with special emphasis on recognizing the wrongs they have done. But the wrongs people have done are usually intertwined with wrongs done against them. So I began hearing about child abuse, rape, tragic deaths, and grave injustices. I took comfort in the belief that just by listening as people tell their stories, I was helping them recover from the past. But as I continued listening to people's traumas and tragedies, I could see that many of these experiences had profound and long-lasting consequences. I began to want to do more than just listen (although I still believe listening long and hard is the vital first step in the process of helping). I began to long for a way to help people experience God's healing from their nightmares.

About that time, I was introduced to the idea of inviting Jesus to be part of our traumatic memories so that he might give us emotional healing. I began to reflect on how Jesus might be the key to helping the people I served recover from their painful past. Then I had a startling experience of this myself.

I was walking up the stairway to the second floor in my home one day, carrying a load of laundry. My one-year-old son was playing halfway up the stairway. I tried to walk around him, but he grabbed on to my legs as I went by. With the laundry basket in my hands and my son wrapped around my feet, I nearly tumbled backward down the stairs. I became irate, putting the basket down and angrily scooping up my son. I took him into his bedroom upstairs and threw him down on his bed, shouting at him *never* to grab someone's feet on the staircase. Immediately, I felt disappointed in myself for having lost my temper at my child. (Something that happened all too often!) But in that instant, something else happened. I looked at how I had thrown my son onto the bed, and the thought came to me that some parents who lose their temper end up shaking their children and breaking their necks! I realized that I had the seeds of rage within me that, if allowed to grow, could produce a situation where I could kill my own child!

I was horrified.

I cried out to God in prayer. Now praying for God's help to control my anger was nothing new—it was perhaps one of my most common prayers. But the vision of me killing my own son made me desperate in a way I had never been before. Tears filled my eyes, and I felt like Jacob who wrestled with God and didn't want to let go until God blessed him. "Lord," I prayed, "would you *please show me* what I need to learn to overcome my anger before it destroys me and the ones I love!"

Then an old, dusty memory appeared immediately in my mind. I was a little boy about ten years old, and my father had told me to go upstairs to bed. I had dillydallied until finally, exasperated, my father had lost his temper and angrily chased me to the stairway. As I scampered up the steps, my dad reached out to swat me with the back of his hand (though I was now out of his reach, and he missed). There the memory ended—with my dad at the bottom of the stairs and I, frightened, at the top. As I thought about it, I could still feel the tension in that memory.

I feel compelled to pause and tell you that my father was a *very good* dad. He was a faithful pastor, a willing provider, and a man devoted to his family (I had six siblings). He almost never lost his temper. In fact, this memory is the only time in my *entire* childhood that I can recall my father flying off the handle.

But there it was—a memory of my own father losing his temper, and it stood out in my mind as if under a spotlight. I asked God if this was somehow connected to my own problem and, if so, what should I do about it. Then I remembered the concept of inviting Jesus into our bad memories. I wasn't at all sure it would help, but I was desperate to try anything, so I prayed, "Jesus, would you please come into this memory, or do whatever needs to be done to help me overcome this wretched anger!"

Immediately, in my memory, I saw Jesus step through a doorway at the bottom of the stairway and stand next to my dad. He reached out his hand and touched my father's shoulder. At that moment, I felt the tension in the memory evaporate.

Peace took over as my father and Jesus sat down together at the bottom of the stairway. But there was more. Jesus looked up at me and motioned with two fingers to invite me down to where they were. I felt safe and peaceful now, so I descended the stairway and sat in the middle, two steps up from my dad and Jesus. And there, the new memory ended.

I was stunned at what I had just seen. But it left me feeling a deep sense of peace. And I had an intuition that, somehow, this was going to help me in my struggle to stay calm with my own kids.

And it did. Without trying any harder, I found myself reacting much more calmly to my children's misbehaviors in the days that followed. And I found myself going back from time to time to the memory of me and my dad and Jesus on the stairway. It was like I could drink from that memory now— drafts of refreshment and peace. To this day, as I write these words, I can still picture that calming scene. For you see, the memory has never gone back to the way it was at first. Jesus is there now. There to stay.

The Treatment Center

Many, though not all, of the stories you are about to read come from my experience as a spiritual counselor at a drug and alcohol treatment center. It was there that I first learned to listen deeply to people in order to help them bring their worst nightmares to light. And it was there that I first learned how to help people bring their traumas to the Lord in prayer. In time, I took what I had learned at the treatment center and put it to work with the Native American people whom I served as well as with my friends and family.

It may be helpful for you to know that the treatment center was not a Christian facility. The program there was based on the twelve steps of recovery used in Alcoholics Anonymous (AA). This is a spiritual program in that it makes reference to God.

But it is not a Christian program in that there is no mention of Jesus Christ or his saving work. What this means on a practical level is that I was free to talk about God as I understand him (which, for me, includes the life and death of Jesus). But I did this not as an authority but simply as another human being. In fact, I believe I had the same standing at the treatment center that every fireman, nurse, businessman, or construction worker in America has with his or her coworkers. We are not spiritual authorities in the marketplace but simply witnesses of what we have seen and heard . . . and come to believe.

One last note: The names of the people in these stories have been changed. But their stories are reproduced here as exactly as my memory would allow. Now let's get going!

Kari: Childhood Sexual Abuse

Kari was about twenty-eight years old. She had shoulder-length sandy brown hair and a warm smile on her round face. We started our conversation by talking about her family as she was growing up. Her father and mother had divorced when she was just a baby. She had grown up with her mother who was an alcoholic and took very little care of Kari.

"There was a lot of drinking going on in my house, and Mom always had her boyfriends around. When things got bad, I would just go over to Grandma's house. She lived pretty close to us, and I always felt safe at Grandma's house."

We got to the subject of abuse, Kari stating that she had been sexually abused when she was five years old. "Have you ever had an opportunity to talk with anyone about that?" I asked.

"I told a counselor once that it had happened."

"You know, Kari," I replied, "the longer I live, the more convinced I am that the only way to get past some of the painful things that have happened to us is to be able to talk about them—to tell the story of what actually happened and how it made us feel. Have you ever actually told anyone what happened?"

"No, not really."

"Would you like to now?"

"Well, I don't actually remember all of it. My mom had a certain boyfriend, and she would let him stay at our house

1

when she was gone for work. Sometimes, he would make me sit with him on his lap, you know, like to read stories to me. But I was always afraid of him. One day, he took me upstairs. And that's all I remember. I don't really know what happened. The next thing I remember is running out of the house. I think I was trying to get to Grandma's house. I still have nightmares about it," she said softly.

"What do you see in the nightmares?" I asked.

"I have this dream. It's always the same. I'm running around the block where this happened. I'm naked, and he's chasing me. I can see Grandmother's house on the other side of the street, but I can never get there . . . Then I wake up shaking and sweating."

"Oh, wow," I said softly. I thought for a moment. "Kari, we've got to get you to Grandma's house!" (I was not at all sure how we were to accomplish that.) "Could we just put this scene on hold for a minute, and could you tell me where you are in terms of spiritual things—what you believe about God? The reason I want to do that is that I think we're going to need his help to get you to Grandma's house."

"Sure," she replied. "Well, I do believe in God. I mean, we never went to church much or anything. But I do believe he's there. I believe he is good and wants to help and protects us . . . that he loves us." She paused. "I guess that's about all."

"OK," I said. "Let's go back to the picture of that nightmare. Is God a part of that picture in any way?"

"No," she replied.

"If we were to put him into that picture, where would he be?"

Kari thought for a moment and then said, "He'd be standing by Grandmother's house."

"Would you like to pray with me and ask God to let you into Grandma's house?" I asked.

Without hesitation, Kari replied, "Yes, I would."

I slid forward in my chair and took hold of Kari's hands.

"How do we do this?" she asked. "I mean do *you* pray or what?"

"Well, I would be happy to pray, but I think it would be good if you pray too."

"OK. It's just that I really don't know much about praying."

"It's pretty simple, really. You just talk to God like you've been talking to me."

"OK, I can do that."

"Do you want to pray first or shall I?" I asked.

"You go first."

So I prayed. I told God how sad I was that we live in a world where such terrible things can happen to little girls. But I thanked him that he's always there to help us. And I asked him to hear as Kari talked to him now.

Then Kari made her simple prayer. She asked God to let her into Grandmother's house. A holy silence descended to the room where we sat, and we held each other's hands tightly, our heads bowed.

I had no picture in my mind, but I could literally feel, first, the terror Kari had experienced, and then a great sense of relief and safety. I suspected God was rolling the film in Kari's mind to bring the picture to a better ending. After a few moments, my eyes still closed, I asked, "Kari, where are you now?"

Through the tears, she replied, "I'm in Grandmother's house."

"Are you alone?" I asked.

"No," she said. "I'm in Grandma's arms."

Now there were enough tears for both of us. And in my heart, I thanked God for taking care of his little child.

Note: I had a chance to talk to Kari again two months after this conversation and prayer. I asked her about the nightmare that she said she had experienced two or three times a week for the past twenty years. Kari stated that since praying about this experience, she had not had that nightmare again but was sleeping soundly now.

ℰↃ ℭℛ

Kathy: Childhood Trauma

"I had kind of a yucky childhood," said Kathy. "Then I was raped when I was fifteen. I think I should go to one of those rape support groups or something. Now I'm in an abusive relationship with my husband. I kind of rationalize it because he only beats me when he's been drinking, but . . ." she trailed off.

I thought for a moment. "All three of those things are very important," I said. "Your most pressing matter is probably the abuse by your husband. But could I suggest we take a while and talk about the first two things, your childhood and the rape, and then come back to the abuse."

"OK," replied Kathy. "Well, my dad was kind of the typical absent father—there physically but not emotionally. I guess my mom was kind of absent too. I know I was always mad at her because she seemed so wrapped up in Dad and his problems. We lived on a farm, and I wanted to get involved in things at school. I wanted to be in band and basketball, but they could never drive me to those things because Dad was always drunk. So I joined the typical girl things—FHA." She paused.

"But your heart was not in it," I said.

"No. I remember I always wanted to take piano lessons. And my grandpa could have driven me there. But Mom said Dad wouldn't like it. That's all—Dad wouldn't like it."

"Why not?"

"She said people would wonder why Grandpa was always driving me there, why *Dad* wasn't. And it would make him look bad."

"So your folks were more concerned about their own image than about you."

"Oh yeah! My mom was always very concerned about what other people were thinking."

"And they were too wrapped up in themselves to be able to help you realize your dream of playing piano?" Then a dialogue popped into my mind from a movie I'd seen, and I asked, "*Are you a piano player?*"

"Well, I'm an *adult* now, and I know we could squeeze money for lessons out of the budget if we tried, but—"

"You're not answering my question. *Are* you a piano player?"

She looked at me timidly and then gazed at the floor. After a moment, she said tentatively, "Well, yes, I suppose that you would have to say that I am."

"Then say it," I urged.

"I *am* a piano player." The words seemed to produce a certain relief. "You know," Kathy said, "I just know that learning to play the piano is something I want to do, something I *have to* do, before I die."

"I'll look forward to hearing you play someday," I said with a smile.

We paused and took a few good breaths. "Is there anything else from your childhood that you'd like to talk about?" I asked.

"Actually, there is one thing," she replied. "I don't know if it's one memory or two. But I remember a time when I was in my crib. Dad was yelling at Mom and pushing her around. I remember seeing Mom lying on the floor. And I remember that she was threatening to call Dad's father if he didn't stop."

"Excuse me," I said, "but you were *how* old here?"

"Well, I must have been under two years old 'cause Mom said we were in the crib till two."

"I just find it *very* interesting that at that young age, you remember not only what you *saw* but also what you *heard* and *understood* as well!"

"Yeah. I guess that is kind of amazing, isn't it? Well, anyway, now comes the weird part. You know how you always hear people talking about disassociation—when you leave your body? Like sometimes when people are dying and they float up to the ceiling and look down on what is happening? Well, I remember looking up into the corner of the ceiling . . . and then

I left my body and went up there. I don't know why I would do that."

"It makes sense to me. That was a pretty scary situation you were in. Especially for a little tot!"

"Yeah! That's for sure."

"Have you ever talked with anyone else about this experience?"

Kathy shook her head. "I was always afraid people would think I was crazy."

I leaned over and took her hand for a moment. "I don't think you're crazy."

We paused for a moment. "This seems like a very significant experience in your life, Kathy. And I don't want to just leave it. But could we put it on pause for just a few minutes because I'd like to kind of switch subjects and have you tell me what you think about God. What kind of experiences have you had with that realm? What do you think he's like?"

"Sure. Well, I've always believed in God." Kathy spoke for a few minutes about her faith. She believed that Jesus died on the cross for us. But that faith had gotten pretty much swallowed up in legalism (all the things she was told she *had* to do and must not do). "I know I'm supposed to believe in God's grace, but I don't really know what grace is," she said with misty eyes. She paused and thought. "You know, I've always said that I believe God loves me . . . but I really *don't*. I see that now."

"How about if we go back to that experience as a little child. Have you ever thought of God as part of that picture?" I asked.

"No, I guess I haven't."

"How about if we think about that for a minute. Was he there . . . anywhere?"

"Well, yeah. I mean he's everywhere. I guess I just never thought of him as being there before."

"So where is he in that picture?" I asked. She sat quietly, thinking for some time. I wondered if I should say how I saw it in my mind, so I said very softly, "I see him up in the corner."

She looked at me with a strange combination of relief and realization. "So that's why he took me up there!"

The sentence hit me like a ton of bricks, and I closed my eyes as tears of relief and gratitude poured out. I remember thinking, *Wait a minute. She's the one who's supposed to be crying over this.* When I finally opened my eyes, I saw that she *was* crying. I took hold of her hands as the tears streamed down her cheeks, and I asked, "Do you want to talk to God about this?"

"Yes." She nodded. "Oh, Lord," she said, "I never realized you were there! It was so scary!" Kathy was sobbing now, and I knelt by her chair to hold her while she cried. "Thank you that you were there for me!" She prayed between the tears.

When we had both finished crying and settled back into our chairs, Kathy looked at me. Her countenance was shining. "You know what? I'm not scared anymore!"

After a break, Kathy and I processed what we'd just gone through together.

"I was thinking," I said, "that this is very good news for your situation of abuse with your husband. Because, in a way that I don't fully understand, I think evil feeds on fear."

"Yes!" she said, nodding vigorously.

"Can you explain that to me?" I asked. "How do those two—fear and abuse—relate to each other?"

"Well, it's like this. When you're being abused, you know you should get out of there. But you're so afraid that he'll come after you. And that fear keeps you from doing anything."

"So the fear immobilizes you."

"Yep."

"Well, how do you look at that situation now?"

Kathy thought for a minute. "Well, now I know I can make it on my own. I don't have to stay there if he keeps doing it."

After a few more moments of conversation, I asked, "Kathy, how about the rape? Is there anything you want to talk about related to that?"

"Not now." Kathy smiled. "You know," she said, "I have been afraid of so many things in my life. And I always tried to deal with the fear, but . . ." She struggled to find the words to express her thoughts.

"But it's like you could never get to the taproot of the fear before? And now that root has been broken?" I offered.

"That's a very good way of putting it!" She smiled.

"Kathy," I said, "now that you've seen Jesus just take you to him back in that memory, do you know what *grace* is?"

Now it was her turn to get hit by the emotional ton of bricks. Leaning back, she closed her eyes and began to sob. Through the tears of joy, she said, "Yes!" And then, "I love you so much, Jesus!"

Note: As part of her continuing recovery, Kathy's counselor put her in touch with people who could give her additional help with the aftermath of rape and domestic abuse.

ഇ ൙

Mike: Child Abuse

When Mike stepped into my office, he seemed nervous. I thought it might be the standard nervousness everyone has when meeting someone new, but I was to discover it had a deeper root. We began talking and eventually got to the subject of Mike's childhood. Mike's dad wasn't around when he was growing up. He had been raised by his mother.

"What was your mom like?" I asked.

"Well, Mom drank a lot. And when she drank, she got pretty mean. She'd hit me . . . bite me. I just tried to stay out of her way. When I came home from school, if she was passed out on the couch, I would try to sneak by her and get upstairs. But if she woke up, she'd come after me."

"She would actually *bite* you?" I said in disbelief.

"Oh yeah! I can remember being thrown around and slammed into the wall. She'd be yelling at me 'You little bastard!'"

I hung my head in sorrow, amazed that we live in a world where a mother would treat her son so cruelly.

"People think I'm nervous," said Mike, his eyes darting this way and that. "But actually, I think I'm still in shock!"

"I don't doubt it one bit!" I concurred. "Mike, could I switch topics for a minute? Where are you with God?"

"God. Well, that's been kind of up and down with me," Mike replied. Then after a pause, he said, "Honestly, I know he's always been with me."

"Then I have another question for you, Mike. Where was God when your mom was beating you up?"

"Where was God then?" Mike said pensively. "Well, that's a hard one."

"Could I suggest an idea?" I proposed. "Could it be that God was there taking the hits right along with you, suffering that same unjust punishment that you were getting?"

"I've never thought of *that*," Mike said slowly.

"A lot of people's idea of God is that he is up above, far removed from the rotten stuff we go through. But have you ever seen a picture of Jesus on the cross?"

Mike nodded.

"Well, it seems to me that gives us a new picture of God— one who *suffers*! If I'm to understand the message right, he felt all the cruelty and pain that this whole sinful world can cause. He did it so he could suffer *with* us and *for* us. So to me, it makes sense to see him right there suffering with you."

Mike was obviously interested in this idea.

"Mike, would you like to take a short break and just talk to God about this whole experience?" I asked.

"Yeah, I would," he responded. "But . . . what would I say?"

"Whatever's in your heart."

"OK."

We held hands and bowed our heads. "Lord," Mike said, "thank you that you've always been there . . . And thank you that you even suffered with me when I was getting beat up. It means a lot to me. I guess that's all I want to say." Mike looked up at me and said with a smile, "That felt good!"

We went on to talk about other things and spoke with each other for another hour or so. As our conversation drew to a close, Mike said, "Thanks a lot. This has really helped me a lot!"

"Good," I said. "May I ask what's been the most helpful?"

"That part about God being with me even when I was a little boy with my mom. I like that—it's not too difficult for me. He's been there and suffered with me!"

ಸಿ ಅ

DeAnna: No Permission to Feel

Note: Although this conversation did not involve prayer for any particular traumatic memory, it helped me clarify several important issues involved in emotional healing.

I was delighted to have an evening to visit with DeAnna in her home after we had participated in a Bible study at the county jail together. I admired DeAnna for the excellent work she was doing with the inmates—visiting them every Tuesday for Bible study and personally in between as well. DeAnna, a married woman in her midforties, was a mother of two young adult children and had been a Christian since her childhood. I had only known DeAnna for a few months, but she seemed like an exemplary Christian woman to me. So I was somewhat surprised when she said she was struggling with "the mother of all depressions" and had been having suicidal thoughts lately. We talked a bit about my work of trying to help others find God's healing for painful experiences in their past. And we got into talking a bit about DeAnna's childhood.

"My mother was often sick when I was young. I remember once when I was just a little girl my mother telling me that I needed to take care of the others in the family. So that's pretty much become my role in life—I'm the caregiver," said DeAnna.

"And who takes care of you?" I asked.

"Oh, nobody!" she replied. She looked at me with a smile that was partly playful and partly forced. "No, that's the way it is with me. DeAnna has no feelings. At least I've grown accustomed to not expressing any feelings or needs. You see, my father was in the military. Feelings weren't very welcome in my family. They were a sign of weakness."

"Oh, really," I said. "I thought they were a sign of being alive!"

DeAnna smiled at my little gibe and continued. "Well, I was too busy taking care of everyone else to have any feelings. I mean, I couldn't express any feeling because that would hurt those around me, and I couldn't do that. I had to take care of them. So I just stuffed all my feelings inside. And you know what? Now I'm *full*. And that's why I think I'm starting to consider suicide."

"DeAnna, the way I see it, God gave us feelings for one purpose—to be *felt*. And those feelings need to be expressed!"

"But how can I express any of my feelings when I know it will just hurt someone else?"

I was perplexed. "Where did you get this idea that expressing your feelings must hurt someone else?"

"Isn't that the way it goes when people start talking about the way they feel? They end up yelling and saying mean things!"

Then I thought of something a twenty-year-old alcoholic named Chad had told me at the treatment center the week before. He had told me how his initial reaction to everything was *anger*. But at the treatment center, he had been learning to take time and think quietly about the experiences that happened to him. As he took time in quiet reflection, he came to realize and identify the true feelings that were behind the anger. Under the hard veneer of anger, there were soft feelings like hurt, fear, worry, and disappointment. He said if he expressed the immediate anger, he ended up hurting people. But if he took time to sink down to the soft feelings just below the surface and expressed *those* to people, they responded warmly and caringly. So I explained this to DeAnna. She thought about it.

"So it's not the actual feeling itself that hurts others but only the hard veneer of anger that we put over our real feelings," she reflected.

"I think that's it," I affirmed.

"Well, I've got plenty of anger. I would even call it *rage*."

"Yeah. And an old Indian friend of mine named Harry said there are four stages to that hard veneer. First, there's anger. Then that grows into rage. From there, it becomes hatred. And if it's not checked, it ends in self-hatred. And there, we're talking suicide."

"That's right," agreed DeAnna. Then thoughtfully, she added, "But there's one more thing between the hatred and the suicide, and that's indifference."

"Ahh . . . You just don't care anymore."

"Yup. That's why you have so many peaceful people committing suicide." A pause. "There was one time, actually, that I did express my real feelings. It was just after I had gotten my divorce from Jim. I was going to a counselor, and she told me I needed to give myself permission to be *real*—to express what I really felt and to act on what I really thought. I told her that's the one thing I couldn't do. So we agreed that *she* would give me the permission to be real. And when I acted on that, it was incredible! I actually *played* with my two kids and *enjoyed* playing with them. I had amazing energy—I could get up at four o'clock in the morning to shovel the snow off the driveway. I was happy and creative. But it didn't last."

"What happened to change all that?"

"Well, my counselor got sick, and so I was never able to meet with her again. But for nine months, I just kept reminding myself she had given me permission to be real. And things continued to go well. So well, in fact, that Jim started to get real with *himself*. Our divorce, (which was all my idea) was a very smooth one, and Jim still came around every day to see the kids and things.

When we were both real with ourselves, we ended up being highly attracted to each other again. So after nine months, we were remarried. And you know, almost immediately, I reverted back to my old ways—stuffing my feelings and doing what others expected of me. So what do you make of that! Did God give me those nine months just to show me what I could never really have?"

I laughed a cruel, devilish laugh, and we both smiled. "Come on, DeAnna," I said. "Listen to what you're saying. You're describing hell! Would God withhold from us the thing we long for the most and then just dangle it out there like a carrot on a stick to forever torture us with the reminder of what we can't have?"

"Well, why didn't it last then?"

I puzzled for a moment. "DeAnna, when you got divorced, were you taking a giant step away from your extended family, your church, everything that meant conventionality for you?"

"Yes, I sure was."

"And when you got remarried, you stepped back into the world that you had left behind—leaving the world of freedom to be yourself. And you were once again swallowed up by the expectations of others."

"I guess that would be true. And it happened almost at once!"

"Where has God been in all this?" I asked. "I mean, which DeAnna does God like most, the free and playful and energetic DeAnna or the DeAnna that stuffs her real self inside so she can take care of everybody else but all the while is withering and dying inside?"

"Well, now that you mention it, there is one more thing about those nine months when I had permission to be real. I felt . . . no, I *was* enveloped in the love of God. I experienced his love for me so strongly! And I found myself really loving other people too, even people I had disliked before. It was amazing!"

"So what you're telling me is that when you were real with yourself—what you really felt and thought—God was all over the canvas of your life."

"Big time!"

"DeAnna, that seems to agree with the picture of Christ that I see in the Gospels. Who were the people who were attracted to Jesus? The hookers and the outcasts, humble fishermen and everyday people—the kind of people who are *real*. But the religious big shots that put up a good front on the *outside*—they couldn't stand him. You see, DeAnna, if I'm reading the Gospels right, it is precisely when we are real—real with our hurts, our fears, our hopes, as well as our dark side, our pride, our bitterness—it is precisely then and *only* then that Christ can work in us . . . or flow through us to others.

"The reason I think this is so significant, DeAnna, is that you have lived your life based on a pattern of stuffing your feelings that was more or less dictated to you by your parents—your most important authority. I'm not surprised that you can't *by yourself* overrule their authority and give yourself permission to be real. But I think you *can* go over their heads to a higher authority. You see, if *Christ* gives you the permission to be real, to be the person God made you to be with all your unique thoughts and *feelings* and dreams, then who can tell you otherwise? Not your military dad. Not the people you work with. Not anybody! God said you have permission to feel!'"

"But that sounds so selfish!"

"Well, that is a very real concern. Nothing is more destructive than selfishness or more important to walk away from. But let me sketch out something for you about how feelings and actions relate." I took a pencil and wrote out the following chart on a piece of stationery DeAnna gave me:

Feelings	Actions
Spontaneous	Planned
Individual	Mutual
Unique	In common
Morally neutral	Good or bad

"You see, DeAnna, I don't believe it's selfish simply to admit that we feel something." I took hold of her arm and squeezed it firmly. "Are you selfish because you feel that? No! All that means is that you have nerves. I guess I think your soul has nerves too. And it's not selfish just to admit that you felt something. But that is just the first step! Next comes the question of what will you *do* in response to your feelings—what *action* will you take. And here's where things can get nasty and people can get selfish."

"But the initial feeling is not in itself wrong or selfish."

I shook my head. "Feelings are morally neutral. God will hold us morally accountable for our actions. But for our feelings, he will . . . just *hold* us."

"Oh, I like that!" smiled DeAnna. "How did that go? For our actions, God will hold us accountable—"

"But for our feelings, he will simply *hold* us," I completed. "DeAnna, would you like to pray with me and ask *Christ* to give you permission to be *real*, to express your real feelings, and be the unique person God made you to be?"

"I think so."

We joined hands and bowed our heads. "Lord Jesus," DeAnna prayed, "I have lived for so long, trying to do everything for everybody else and so afraid of hurting them, but I can't take it any longer. I think I really need this permission from you to be real with myself. So I'm asking you to give me the permission to be honest with what I really feel but still loving toward others in the things I do. Help me, Jesus. Amen."

DeAnna looked up at me, her eyes clear and bright. "So now what do I do?"

"What do you feel like doing?" I asked.

"I know!" she said and got up and ran out the door. I saw her fly out to her flower garden. She returned with a handful of daisies. "There!" she said when she reentered the room. "Picking daisies at midnight—just because I felt like it!"

Note: I stayed in touch with DeAnna in the days that followed. Whenever I talked with her, I would be sure to ask, "Did Christ give you permission to be real today?" She would usually say something like "Well, I had to remember several times to ask him for permission to be real. But every time I did, he gave it to me. When I'm honest about what I really feel, he helps me to do what I really should. And it feels great!"

∾ ❧

John: Parents' Violence

John was a small man and slightly built. He had short brown hair and quiet eyes behind his wire-rimmed glasses.

As we began our conversation, he told me how his parents had both died when he was young. "My father was an alcoholic and died of a bleeding ulcer when I was ten. Then my mother died when I was about eleven."

"What happened to your mom?" I asked.

"She came home drunk one night, fell down the stairs, and died. So after that, I went to live with my uncle and aunt."

"Sounds like things weren't exactly easy for you as a boy," I offered.

"No, it wasn't exactly pretty living with alcoholic parents. My dad never beat me up or abused me, but I remember times when he would beat my mother. There was blood . . ." His voice trailed off. "It's funny. I can see it all in my mind just as sharp as if it happened yesterday."

When I heard this, I was pretty sure we were dealing with a memory in need of healing. But we hadn't been talking long, and I wasn't sure if John was comfortable enough with me yet to engage in the spiritual process of prayer for healing. Still, I decided to try.

"You know, John, I've been coming to believe that God wants to help us heal from those hurtful memories that remain vivid pictures in our minds. It sounds like this is one of those experiences for you that's been hard to forget."

"Yeah, that's for sure."

I went on to explain to John how I had prayed for God to heal me of a frightening memory from my childhood. "Where are you at with God, John? What do you believe about him?" I asked.

"He's all-loving . . . and powerful. I grew up in the Catholic Church and ended up with a lot of fear about God. But I've kind of rejected that as I've gotten older and done more study. Now I believe that God is only loving. He doesn't have a hateful side," John explained.

We talked more about John's beliefs. While I didn't agree with everything John said, my intention now was mainly to see if John had faith to pray for healing.

"What do you believe about Jesus?" I asked. "Because when I think of asking God to heal a memory, it basically comes down to inviting him to be *with* us in that memory. And to do that, it helps so much to be able to *see* God there with us. I believe Jesus was just that—God on earth in a human body, real and visible here with us. Do you believe that Jesus was the Son of God who came to earth for us?" I asked.

"Yes, I do," John replied.

"Would you like to pray together and invite him to share that memory with you . . . to ask him to help you picture him there with you?"

"Yes, I think I would," John responded.

"I like to hold hands when I pray with someone. Would that be OK?"

John reached out to take my hands.

"Jesus," John prayed, "I'm coming to you for help with this memory of what happened when I was a boy. If you could help me see you there, I'd appreciate it."

"John," I said, "you said that memory was still sharp. Can you see it now?"

"Yes," John replied.

"Would you like to tell me what you see?"

"I'm lying on my bed. Through the door, I can see my mom and dad in the next room by the oil furnace. They're starting to argue and yell at each other. And then my dad starts to hit my mom. Then she's down on the floor, and he's kicking her. There's blood all over her and on the furnace. She's screaming at him to stop. And finally, he quits and walks to their bedroom. I thought my mom might be dead, but she got up after a minute and walked away too."

"How did you feel?"

"Afraid . . . And then after that, I remember thinking, 'Why me?! Why do I have to see this!'"

"If we were to picture Jesus there with you, where would he be? Can you see him there?"

"He's standing by the foot of my bed."

"What does he look like?" I asked.

"He's wearing a white gown, just like in all the pictures. And he has long flowing hair."

"How does it feel with him there?"

"Good. I feel . . . protected!" John exclaimed.

I hoped that John could feel the warmth of Jesus's touch, so I asked, "Can you picture Jesus coming over and taking your hand?"

John paused for a moment.

"I see him walking over to me and putting his hand on my head as I'm lying on the bed. It's like he's filling in as a parent for me. He's letting me know that what's going on doesn't have to keep hurting me. I still don't know why it happened, but he lets me know that someday I'll understand. And in the meantime, he's like a buffer between what my parents are doing and me. I feel . . . protected."

After another pause, I asked, "Is that a good place for this memory to end?"

"Yes," said John, opening his eyes. "That was *really* nice. I didn't know I could ask Jesus to do something like that!"

Is This Really That New?

M any times when I pray with people and we see Jesus with them in their traumatic memories, they comment on what a new idea this is for them. But is it really that novel?

On the bedroom wall of my son, Michael, hung a painting that showed a young man standing at the wheel of a sailing ship amid stormy winds and waves. Jesus is standing behind the young man with one hand on his shoulder and the other pointing the way ahead. The message is clear: let Jesus be your guide.

On a meeting-room wall at the camp where I am currently ensconced to work on this book is a beautiful tapestry of Jesus. He is sitting on a rock in a wooded area, and a little boy is leaning on his lap and looking up into his eyes. In the camp director's office is another painting of Jesus enthusiastically playing soccer with a bunch of kids.

Aren't all these artists doing what artists have done for centuries—using their imagination and artistic skills to communicate the message that Jesus is with us at all times and in all places? Are we doing anything differently when we pray about painful moments in our past and ask the Lord, "Can you help me see you there?"

Of course, we should plainly acknowledge that we are employing our imagination at these times. But that does not mean we are coming up with something that is *imaginary* (i.e., not real). In fact, in view of the promises of God, I would say that our imagination is taking us *closer to reality* in those situations, not farther away from it.

If anything, maybe we're giving a new twist to an old theme. It's the theme articulated by Matthew when he wrote of Jesus's birth: "And they will call him Immanuel—which means, 'God with us'" (Matthew 1:23).

℘ ℭ

Karissa: Poor Discipline

Karissa was a twenty-eight-year-old young woman with a very hip, multicolored haircut. We had met to talk about her recovery from drug addiction.

"My dad divorced my mom when I was about four," began Karissa. "Mom got remarried, but I never got along very well with my stepdad. He was very harsh with me. I remember a time when I got whacked on the hand because I wanted a second glass of milk."

Karissa went on to describe how she had grown older and begun to rebel against her parents. "I got involved with the using crowd. Then I got pregnant, but the baby's dad didn't want to take care of my son. So for a while, I thought it would be just me and my baby. Then I met my current boyfriend. I didn't think any guy would be interested in me since I had a kid. But he took the whole package. He really is good with my son. He loves to play with him and even tries to discipline him when he does something bad. But I kind of undermine that. I mean, my boyfriend will give him time out in his room, but I always let him out. I know it's not good. I know my son runs all over me, but I just can't bear to leave him in his room!"

"Why's that?" I asked, perplexed.

"I don't know. Maybe it goes back to the way I was treated when I was young. They would always send me to my room, and I hated it."

"What kind of things did you do that got you sent to your room?"

"Just stupid stuff. I don't know. I didn't say the right thing or say it in just the right way. Any little thing would get me sent to my room. I was always so afraid! I would sit by the door and just wait for Mom to come and get me."

Karissa paused for a moment and then went on. "One time, I felt something touch me when I was alone in my room. It was like cold fingers that went right through me. I don't know what that was."

"How did it make you feel?" I asked.

"Scared."

I felt that right now, Karissa might be a little scared that her experience seemed wacky. So I tried to reassure her. "There're a lot of things I don't completely understand in life, but I do believe there are spiritual beings in this world. It sounds to me like you might have felt the presence of something like that. And fear is the trademark of the devil and all his crew."

"You know, we found out later that there was a little boy who had been killed by his father in that house before we moved in. And it kind of felt like little hands that were touching me. I thought maybe it was the spirit of that little boy, and he was lonely."

"Well, that's more than I know," I admitted. "What I am sure of is that anything that produces fear in our lives needs to be dealt with. You know, just this morning, I was reading in the Bible in the first chapter of Mark's biography of Jesus. One of the first things that Jesus did in chapter 1 was to kick out a demonic spirit that was harassing a man. To me, that says that one of the most important things Jesus came to do was to free us from the evil influence of bad spirits." I paused for a moment and then asked Karissa, "What do you believe about Jesus?"

"Oh, I believe everything about him. I mean, that he was sent to save us and all the miracles and things he did—I believe it all."

"The reason I ask is because I often find it to be very healing to ask Jesus to go back with us into painful memories and be there to help us heal from the effects those experiences had on us. Can you still picture yourself alone and scared in that room?"

"Yes, I can."

"Would you like to pray and ask Jesus to be with you in that memory?"

"Yes, I would," said Karissa.

"I like to join hands when I pray with someone. Would that be OK?"

"Sure," said Karissa, reaching out to take my hands as I pulled my chair closer.

"Go ahead," I said to Karissa. "Just ask him in your own words."

"Dear Jesus," Karissa prayed, "please be with me when I was a little girl alone in my room. I need your help. I don't want to feel afraid."

"Karissa," I asked, "can you picture yourself alone in that room?"

"Yes."

"How does it look?"

"It's just me by myself. I'm sitting near the door, hoping someone will come and let me out."

"Can you picture Jesus there with you?"

"Yes, I can."

"Where is he?" I asked.

"He's standing right beside me."

"How does it feel to have him there?"

Through the tears that had begun to come, Karissa said softly, "Comfort."

"Does he communicate anything to you, or do you say anything to him?" I asked.

"No, he's just there with me."

I knew this was just a single step in a long journey for Karissa. A small step but an important one!

ℰℭ

Danette: Grief

Danette was a young Native American woman in her late twenties. Her dark curly hair was pulled into a ponytail atop her head, and she had a very athletic look. (I found out later she had dreamed of being a pro basketball player while in high school.) As she began to tell me her life story, she described in saddening detail the bad home life she had growing up.

"My mom drank a lot when I was young. And she got mean when she was drunk. I remember one time when I went into a bar to try and get her to come home. She just yelled at me, so I left. Later when she did come home, she started hitting me with a flyswatter and chased me out of the house and down the driveway. My two younger sisters and I pretty much learned to stay away from home when she was drinking. We'd stay outside during the day and hide in a closet at night . . . We spent a lot of time in that closet."

I made a mental note of this memory of hiding in the closet, thinking that maybe it would be one that Jesus could heal. But I was to find out that the deepest hurt, and the one God would choose to work on, was not a visual memory but a wound of loss and grief.

"Where did you go when your mom chased you out of the house?" I asked.

"To my grandparents' house. Their door was never locked, and we could always go there for some food or a place to sleep. My aunt Margaret lived there too . . . until she died of cancer."

"Was she your mother's sister?"

"Yes. Her older sister."

"How old were you when she died?" I asked.

"Eleven." Danette paused and then her head sank down and she began to cry.

I reached out and put my hand on Danette's. "You loved her a lot, didn't you?"

"She was the only one who ever really loved me."

I allowed Danette to cry for a few moments. "How did she show you her love?"

"She used to buy me little things. But mostly, it was just in the way she talked to me. She knew what was going on at my house. I know she knew. But we didn't talk much about it. She would ask me about all kinds of things. And I could tell her anything. She never had any children of her own, so I guess she kind of treated me like her own . . . since nobody else was taking care of me. I felt so alone after she died!"

Danette was quiet for a long time, and I felt something needed to be done but wasn't sure what. "Would you like to pray and thank God for your aunt Margaret?"

"Yes, I would!" exclaimed Danette.

I slid my chair closer, and we joined hands to pray. "Go ahead," I said.

We sat with our heads bowed for a few moments, but Danette said nothing. Finally, I asked her, "Would I be right in guessing there may be some kind of block between you and God?"

"Yeah, I guess so," replied Danette. "I guess I've just always had a hard time with why he let her die when I needed her so much. I used to pray before that happened. But after her death, I just kind of quit."

"So her death became an obstacle between you and God."

"I guess so."

"Danette, can I tell you the only thing that helps me get around this kind of obstacle?"

"Yes, please!" she responded.

"Well, I think we all start with a picture of God as the one who is up there somewhere controlling all the stuff that goes on down here. You know, 'This person's going to die today. This one will get well. A storm's going to happen here today' and so on. And you know, I can get pretty mad at a god like that when I see all the rotten things that go on."

Danette nodded.

"But everything changes for me when I see the pictures of Jesus on the cross. You see, he's the only person who's ever claimed to be God in the flesh, and people took him seriously. Others have claimed to be God, but most of them are in psych wards," I said with a smile. "Of course, it helped that he could walk on water and heal blind men with the touch of his hand!

"But then, the Bible says that when he was only thirty-three years old, he was secretly arrested, falsely accused, and nailed onto a cross! What's up with that! God suffers! And his friends later explained in the Bible that Jesus was actually carrying all the world's sin on himself at the cross. Could I show you a verse from the Bible about that?"

"Sure," responded Danette.

We looked at 1 Peter 2:24: "He bore our sins in his body on the tree."

"Sin is basically everything that's wrong in the world. So when the Bible says Jesus took all our sins on the cross, it's saying he suffered the pain of all the bad things that have ever happened in this world. Your aunt's death was part of the sin in the world. God never intended people to die! That only happened once people turned their back on God and began going against his will. So part of what Jesus suffered on the cross was the pain of your aunt's death . . . and the pain of a little eleven-year-old girl whose heart was broken when Margaret died. I can be pretty mad at a god who remains up there while we go through all the suffering down here. But I have a hard time being angry with God when I see that he *shared* all our sufferings on the cross. That's the one thing that gets me around obstacles like this one. What do you think about that, Danette?"

"It makes a lot of sense when you explain it like that! But I . . . I didn't know that back then. I just felt all alone."

"Have you ever read the 'Footprints' poem?" I asked.

"Yeah."

"There was only one set of footprints in the darkest time. Why wasn't he there? And God says, 'No, I didn't leave you, I *carried you*!'"

Danette sat thinking for a while. "So he *was* there!"

"Danette, would you like to try talking to God again about your aunt's death?"

"Yes, I would, but . . . I don't know what to say."

I showed Danette Psalm 62:8 where God invites us to "pour out our hearts to Him."

"Just let your heart speak," I said.

We bowed our heads again.

"God," Danette began, "it hurt so much when Aunt Margaret died. And I didn't know what to do! I felt so all alone. But I know I wasn't alone. I'm sorry for turning my back on you. And I ask you now to help me. Please take this pain away and help me get over my aunt's death . . . Amen."

We sat back in our chairs and looked at each other.

"How does that feel?" I asked.

"It feels . . . good. Really good! I feel kind of calm." Danette sat still for a moment and then exclaimed, "Wow, I can breathe again! It's like there was something stuck right there for a long time"—Danette tapped on the center of her chest—"and now it's gone, and I can finally breathe! Oh my god, I feel like I want to smile!"

"That's OK!" I responded. "You can smile!"

Danette burst into a big smile. Then she shook her head in amazement and sat pensively for a moment. "I've never felt like this," she said.

"Is it . . . peace?" I asked.

"Yes," she said, nodding. "I think I'd just like to soak it in for a minute, if you don't mind."

We both paused and sat for a moment in a silence that was rich and full.

Natalie: Prostitution

Natalie walked into my office at the treatment center. She sat down, somewhat nervously, and began telling me her life story.

"My parents couldn't take care of me, and when I was eight years old, I moved in to live with my auntie."

"How did that go?" I asked.

"Not so good. I had a fourteen-year-old cousin who did some bad stuff." Natalie proceeded to tell me about the sexual abuse she suffered.

Natalie's story wound its way to her older years. "As an adult, I became a prostitute to get money for my crack cocaine habit." She paused, looking down.

"How did that make you feel?" I asked.

"I felt yucky, ashamed, gross," answered Natalie with a twisted expression on her face. There was another pause.

"You know, Natalie, I believe God knows about our gross feelings. Jesus told his followers to baptize people. *Baptizing* just means 'washing,' like we do every day. But with baptism, I believe God washes us *inwardly* where we ourselves can't reach. Our actions bring on those yucky feelings, but only God's action can get rid of them."

"I've been baptized!" said Natalie. "When I was six years old—it was a good feeling."

"Natalie, would you like to pray and ask Jesus to clean out that yucky feeling you have inside when you think of your past?" I offered.

"Yes, I would." Natalie took my hands and prayed, "Jesus, please come down and clean out this yucky feeling and make me feel good and clean inside."

With my head still bowed, I asked, "Would you like to picture Jesus cleaning away all that yucky stuff?"

"Yes, I would," answered Natalie.

"Was there a time you felt especially yucky? Maybe when your cousin did that to you? Was that the first time?"

"Yes."

"Can you picture Jesus coming to you there, wearing a white robe, and speaking gently to you, saying, 'Don't be afraid'?"

"Yes," said Natalie softly.

I went on describing the scene that I saw unfolding in my mind. "And can you picture him holding your hand and taking you away to a grassy hill with a pool of clear water and a trickling waterfall? And he says to you, 'You wash in this pool, and I will wash out all the yucky stuff in your soul.' So you swim in that pool, and when you come out, Jesus hands you a radiant white robe. Dressed in that white robe, you sit on his lap, and he says, 'From now on, when anything happens to you, come to me, and I will take care of it . . . and of *you*.'"

I stopped, and in a moment, Natalie opened her eyes and looked at me. "I could picture *all* that!" she said. "And I feel such relief. It's like the tension inside just disappeared! I never wanted to even face up to what I did as a prostitute. I didn't want to talk about it. But now I just feel relief!"

An Ongoing Process

Someone like Natalie undoubtedly has *reams* of bad memories stored away in her heart. And in time, God will probably want to help her face other memories and experience his healing in them as well.

It probably goes without saying that when we experience a healing moment with God, even if it relates to our absolutely *worst* memory, we still haven't won the battle. We may have done a good day's work, but the battle will be continued in the morning. Satan never gives up, and when he loses one stronghold that he has used to torment us, he will look for another.

But the Good News is that every time Satan drags something up from our past to terrorize us, we can take it to Jesus. If it's a sin, we can confess it. If it's a resentment, we can forgive it. If it's a fear, we can turn it over to his perfect love that casts out fear. No matter what it is, we can welcome his presence into that part of our life, and he will bring us peace. For "He himself is our peace" (Ephesians 2:14). And so, we will be in the ongoing process of renewing our mind and experiencing his good, pleasing, and perfect will. It's a daily battle. But when we know our Champion, the assignment is easy and the load is light.

ഉ൦ൽ

Roger: Recurring Nightmares

Roger was a man in his midforties. He had been talking through his fifth step with me for some time when he mentioned nightmares that had recurred over the period of several years during his childhood.

"From the time I was about age four until I was twelve years old, I had four nightmares that returned maybe once a month or so," said Roger. "In the first one, I woke up during the night, walked down the stairs, and saw a man in a black cloak stealing my mother and father's best silverware.

"In the second dream, I walked down the stairway of our house. On a landing halfway down the steps, my father kept a pair of coveralls hanging on a hook. As I walked past the coveralls, my arm was sucked up into the sleeve of the coveralls. It spun me around and threw me down the stairs into a room that was different than the room that actually existed at the bottom of the stairs. That was the end of that dream. But the last two are the scariest.

"In the third one, I remember looking out a window of our house. As I was standing there, something from behind—I could never *see* anything—lifted me up, and I heard this hideous voice saying, 'We've got you now! We're gonna take you away.' I kicked and struggled to get out of its grasp! Then I would wake up.

"And the fourth was worst of all. In the fourth dream, I woke up in the middle of the night. It was very dark, and in my dream, I went to the window of my bedroom. Looking out the window, I could see my mother and father and my brothers and sisters walking away across the yard under the yard light. I banged on the window and called to them, 'Wait, don't leave without me!' Then I turned and ran down the stairs because I kept my coat in the basement and had to get my coat to go with them. When I came to the landing going to the basement,

I looked down to the bottom of the stairs. There was a man dressed in black standing next to a huge chopping block. He had a large ax in his hand—the kind used for cutting someone's head off. When I saw him down there, I decided I didn't need my coat that badly and turned to run away. But I couldn't move! I couldn't get out of the house. I couldn't get away from him! And that's where the dream ended."

I was unsure whether these dreams, which Roger had so long ago, were having any detrimental effect on his life today. But they seemed rather scary, so I asked, "Roger, would you like to hear about a step that you could take for dealing with those dreams?"

"Yes, I would," Roger replied.

I explained to him how Jesus promised always to be with us, but we often live unaware of him. I asked Roger if he would like to invite Jesus to be a part of that memory of the nightmares he had as a child.

"I would like that," said Roger. "I want to tell you," he went on, "that I actually do believe there is a devil. And I've always felt like he was trying to get my soul somehow—like that man with the chopping block was trying to get my soul."

I responded, "Roger, I agree with you that there really are evil spiritual beings, and they want to destroy us. But Jesus promises that when we walk with him, he has the power to keep us safe from the devil and any other power that would try to destroy us."

Roger and I joined hands to pray, and I began by simply thanking Jesus for always being with us and having the power to protect us.

Then I asked Roger, "When you remember that dream, what scene comes most vividly to your mind?"

"Seeing the man with the ax and the chopping block," replied Roger.

"Can you picture that now?" I asked.

"Yes, I can."

"If you were to picture Jesus as part of that memory, where would he be? Can you imagine him entering that scene?"

"Yes, I can. He's leading me out of the house," said Roger. Now the tears were coming to his eyes.

"We're going across the yard towards my family," Roger continued.

"Is he saying anything to you or touching you in any way?" I asked.

"He has his hand on me," said Roger.

And now the tears flowed freely and became sobs of relief.

"What does he look like?" I asked Roger.

"I don't see his face. Actually, what I see is my own face, and it's smiling. It's smiling!"

"Do you see your family?"

"Yes," said Roger. "Jesus is taking me toward them."

"Do they receive you?" I asked.

"Yes, we're all hugging now, and we're in the light. It's daylight now, not night."

"Is this a good place for that memory to end?" I asked Roger.

"Yes," he replied.

When we finished praying and I looked at Roger's face, there was a look of wide-eyed amazement and deep relief revealed in his countenance.

"Thank you!" he said. "That feels so much better."

After taking a short break, we talked more. Roger expressed to me his sadness for how far and how often he had gotten offtrack with God. He expressed his desire to recapture that childlike trust that a four-year-old has. So we took some time to pray. Roger asked God for help to trust him with all his heart and to follow him consistently in his life.

80 CB

32

Calvin: Parental Neglect

Calvin grew up in a large family with four brothers and four sisters. As he began telling me his life story, he related how his mom was usually home, but his dad was always gone working. I wondered if Calvin didn't feel some pain regarding his father's noninvolvement in his life. But at first, Calvin talked about it as if it were just another fact of life—his dad had to be gone. As we talked on, however, he hit on a memory of his parents that seemed vitally important.

"I remember one day when my mom and dad were leaving home," Calvin said. "They got in the car to drive away, and I ran after them, yelling at them to come back. I ran down a dusty gravel driveway, but I couldn't catch them. I couldn't make them stop. I fell down with my face in the gravel, crying. I must have fallen asleep there because I remember waking up sometime later with my face still in the gravel."

As I listened to Calvin describe this memory, I thought how painful it would have been if that had happened to *me* as a child. I made a mental note that this was a memory in need of healing. We talked on for some time and got to the point of discussing Calvin's relationship with a woman.

"We've lived together for twenty years and have three children together," Calvin explained. "For most of those years, the relationship had been pretty bad—a lot of fighting and making hell for each other."

But Calvin expressed how much he wanted to make a family life that was good and workable and wholesome. I asked him if he would like to pray together with me and ask for God's help to restore his family. He nodded eagerly.

"Yes, I would," he replied.

In prayer, as Calvin asked for God's help, I heard him say, "All I want, God, is what I've always wanted, for someone to love me so that I could love them back."

When Calvin finished praying, I said to him, "Calvin, as I heard you pray those words—that you've always just wanted somebody to love you—I thought back to that memory you shared when your parents drove off and left you lying facedown in the dirt. That's all you wanted back then too, wasn't it? Just that someone would love you." Calvin nodded with a sad smile on his face.

"Calvin, you have spoken to me about your faith in Jesus. Is it true that you believe Jesus has always been with you?"

"Yes," Calvin said. "I believe he has. It's just that, at times, I didn't know anything about him—like back when I was a boy."

"Would you like to pray with me and ask God to help you picture Jesus there with you, loving you when you needed it the most?"

"Yeah, let's do that," Calvin said.

We bowed our heads and joined hands. I said, "Calvin, can you picture yourself there on the gravel road?"

"Yes."

I paused for a moment and then said, "Calvin, can you see Jesus there with you?"

He said, "Oh, yes, I'm already seeing him there."

"What does he look like?" I asked.

"He's standing right next to me," Calvin replied. "He's wearing a robe, and he has long hair and a beard."

"Can you picture Jesus reaching down and picking you up out of the dirt and enfolding you in his arms and holding you close to himself?"

Now the tears flowed freely out of Calvin's eyes, and he said, "Yes, I can."

Tears were flowing from my eyes too. I continued in prayer, "Lord Jesus, thank you that you came to this earth and became one of us for no other reason than to reach down and lift us out of the dirt. Thank you that no matter what wrongs we've done, no matter what sins we carry on our backs, none of it stops you from picking us up and holding us to yourself in an embrace of love."

We concluded our prayer, and Calvin reached out and took a Kleenex to wipe the tears away. Calvin was a big man who'd worked much of his life in construction and other "manly" jobs.

"I guess I'm nothing but a big baby when it comes to the Lord," he said with a smile.

I wanted to reassure him, so I said, "I bet you remember the words that Jesus spoke when he said we must become like a child to enter into the kingdom of heaven? Calvin, I think there's a little child within *each one of us* that wants, just like you said, *simply to be loved*. And that is what Jesus does for us—better than anyone else can!"

ℰℭ

Marilyn: Violent Sexual Experience

Marilyn sat in the chair in my office, nervously bouncing her knee. I asked if she was cold, but she said she was quite comfortable. Still, I offered her a blanket that lay decoratively on a nearby couch, and she took it gladly, tucked her legs underneath her, and wrapped it around herself. Marilyn's long chestnut hair was beautiful, but her furtive eyes, ringed in black mascara, had an ominous look to them. I sensed that Marilyn had been through some *very* difficult things and was glad to see her get the extra security of being wrapped in a blanket.

Marilyn began to tell me about her life.

"My father left my mother when I was very young. After that, she had a succession of boyfriends. Most were no good. Some were violent. Us kids got abused just about every way there is."

"Would you like to tell me what you remember from those early days?" I asked.

"Are there certain scenes that stand out in your memory?"

"I remember one time when my mother got beaten by her boyfriend. She was in a car, and he was slamming her head against the steering wheel. That was one of the first times I disassociated. Not long after that was when evil entered into my life."

I took note of Marilyn's comment about disassociating (temporarily blacking out or taking a perspective away from our body due to extreme emotional pain). I was also struck by her comment about evil coming into her life, so I queried, "Do you remember a specific event that brought evil into your life?"

Marilyn nodded. "What happened in the closet, I've been trying to deal with that for years!"

"Marilyn, when I have troubling memories, I sometimes pray for God to help. Where are you at as far as God?"

"Well, I never knew much about God when I was a girl. We never went to church or anything. But in 1987, I gave my life to Christ, and that helped me a lot. I actually was doing really well—I got married, started my own business (a secondhand shop), had two kids with my husband, and all of us had the same name on the mailbox! I haven't left God or anything, but last year, we lost a couple family members and 80 percent of my husband's business, and we didn't handle the grief well. We let it come between us. I think we started blaming each other for our pain. Then he left, and I began drinking again."

I talked with Marilyn about Jesus's suffering on the cross, how he "bore our griefs and carried our sorrows" (Isaiah 53:4). "So if I understand the message of the scriptures right, every one of your painful memories are *part* of what Jesus suffered on the cross. Or you could flip it around and look at it the other way. Jesus suffered on the cross because he was there with you when you were a child. *He was with you* in your suffering. Just like he is with us right here in this room, although we can't see him. But it often helps me a lot to think back to my most painful memories and picture him there *as he really was*! I just pray,

'Lord, help me see you there.' Would you like to try that with the memory of when your mom was getting beaten up?"

"Oh boy. It's really hard for me to go back to those times." Marilyn paused. "OK, let's give it a try."

"I like to join hands when I pray. Are you OK with that?"

"Sure," Marilyn said as we pulled our chairs closer and joined hands.

"How should I do this?" Marilyn asked, looking into my eyes with fear in her own.

"Why don't you just talk to God about what happened and ask Jesus, 'Help me see you there!'"

"Oh, Jesus, you know how much horrible stuff there is in my past. But I want your help to face it. Help me see you there when my mother was getting beaten up."

Marilyn paused, so I asked, "Marilyn can you picture that scene with your mother?"

"Yes. I'm a little girl about five years old. I'm standing beside the car, and my mother is in the driver's seat. Her boyfriend is next to her, and he's slamming her head into the steering wheel. There is blood on the windshield and driver's window. Then I ran to the neighbor's house, and they called the ambulance. They came and took my mom away to the hospital. That's about all I remember."

"If Jesus were to become visible in that scene, where would he be? Can you picture him anywhere?"

"I see him standing beside me next to the car."

"How does it feel to have him there?"

"I really can't feel anything because my feeling part has left me."

I was confused by this statement but then remembered what Marilyn had said about disassociating. I decided to try to help Marilyn reconnect with herself.

"Marilyn, what if Jesus were to stoop down to that little girl and say, 'I know that part of you has left because you've been so frightened by what has happened. But it's OK for you to come back now. I'm here to help you.' How would that be?"

Marilyn let out a shriek that startled and scared me. She pulled her hands away from me and sat back, pulling the blanket up to her chin. "No! Because then, she would have to face the pain of all the beating and sexual abuse and prostitution that would be part of the years ahead!"

I was shaken. I began to think I had tried to do too much too fast. So I backed off a bit, saying, "OK, Marilyn. Maybe I've jumped the gun a little here. Maybe Jesus knows that when a child has run off because she's scared, you don't tell her to come back. You just start doing something fun, and she'll come back when *she* feels safe. How about if we just talk through some more of the things that have happened to you and let that little girl come back when she's ready?"

Marilyn showed evident relief. "That would be better," she replied.

So we talked through some more of Marilyn's experiences. I listened as Marilyn described how she had gotten married to a very troubled man who had, at one point, beaten her so hard, he fractured her skull. "Then he took me, bleeding, and my daughter to an old abandoned warehouse where he . . . did things to my daughter and me. The next morning, I was able to talk him into letting me leave the warehouse, and I got to a Laundromat. I called 911, and the police came and arrested him. That was the last I had to do with him!" I listened to what Marilyn was saying, but my mind kept going back to what she had said about the time evil first entered her life.

"Marilyn," I said at one pause, "you mentioned earlier about something that happened in a closet when evil first entered your life. Do you want to tell me about that?"

"Oh . . . I've been trying to deal with that for a long time . . . OK, it was in a closet at my uncle's house. He had stash of really bad magazines. I mean, these made *Playboy* look tame. I used to go into a closet at his house and turn on the light and look at them. I also . . . did things to myself. It actually hurt, but for some reason, I kept doing it."

"Marilyn, would you like to pray and ask Jesus to come into that memory and rescue you from what went on in that closet?"

"Yes, I would."

We bowed to pray. "Oh, Jesus," Marilyn began, "I need your help with what happened to me back in the closet!" Tears began to come, and Marilyn's voice quivered. "It was the beginning of so many bad things for me. Please help me, Jesus!"

"Marilyn, can you see Jesus standing with you there in that closet?"

"Yes, I can."

"Can you picture him kneeling down beside you and, with a sweep of his hand, all those magazines disappear, and he takes you up in his arm and holds you close to his chest? Can you see that?"

"Yes!" responded Marilyn. The tears were taking on a different character now.

"Can you imagine Jesus picking you up and turning to carry you out of that closet? But you don't come into a room. He carries you right out into a grassy place where the sun is shining brightly. Can you picture that?"

"Yes, I can."

"And can you imagine Jesus carrying you to the edge of a pool of water? It's clear and bright and beautiful. Jesus sets you down so you can swim in that pure, cleansing water. It's refreshing! And as you swim, it's like the water soaks out all the dirt deep inside you so that you feel just clean. As you come out of that pool, Jesus hands you fresh white clothes. In those clothes, you look and feel like a princess! Then Jesus says to you, 'Would you like to meet some other children?' You notice that there are other children playing nearby. So you respond, 'I'll meet them if you'll come with me.' Is that a good way for that memory to end?"

"Yes, very good!"

I talked with Marilyn the next day and asked her how things were going.

"Great!' she replied. "I feel so much more peaceful. I had a few bad memories come to mind last night as I was lying on my bed, but I did just what you told me to do. And I could picture Jesus there with me. It wasn't as big a deal as when we prayed yesterday. I mean, then, I could *see* him! I could smell him! I could *feel* his robe! It wasn't like *that*, but it gave me the same peace. It's so great because I feel like I have a *way* to deal with these memories that I never had before. And, Mark, I have tried millions of times to face what we faced yesterday. But I never could! I have gone to therapists for years. I mean, I knew this stuff was affecting me. It was coming out in my relationships. And the therapists had me listening to tapes and doing visualizations. But I could just never go there! Not until we went there with Jesus."

"Isn't that why we call him Savior?" I replied. "Because he can do for us what we can't do for ourselves!"

ಸಿ ೞ

Brad: Broken Trust

Brad, a man in his midthirties, sat with me in my office one day. As we talked back over his life, Brad made the offhanded comment "I have a hard time trusting people. I don't know why." Then he caught himself. "You know, the truth is I *do* know why."

Brad began to relate a time, back when he was a young boy of about ten, when he found out that his father had been unfaithful to his mother and slept with another woman.

"It really hit me hard," said Brad.

He went on to relate how this experience had affected him throughout his life and made it very hard for him to trust people.

"Do you still think about that experience today?" I asked.

"Oh yeah! I think about it often. Sometimes I get so worked up about it that I end up pacing. I actually get drunk over it sometimes."

As we talked on, Brad admitted that this broken trust was putting a stress on his relationship with the woman he was with today. "Brenda would never do anything like that. She would never be unfaithful to me. I know that. And yet, even though I know it in my head . . ." He paused, groping for words.

"Even though you know it in your head," I suggested, "maybe you still have doubts . . . troublesome feelings in your *heart*."

"Yeah," he said, "that's right."

I could see clearly that the experience of Brad's broken trust in his father was a wound that still hurt him today. Yet I was unsure how God might help Brad to heal from this wound. Unlike so many other experiences I'd prayed about with people, this one didn't seem to have a *visual* side to it. It was, after all, something Brad had *heard* more than seen.

"You know, Brad, it seems to me that this experience has really left a wound in your heart. It's really made it difficult for you to trust people, especially women, the way you want to trust them."

"Yeah, that's for sure," replied Brad.

"Brad, would you like to ask God for help with this—help to overcome your doubt? You see, even though your father let you down very badly when he was unfaithful to your mother, I believe that God himself never lets us down. He is the one person we can go to for help with every need. Does that make sense to you?"

"Yes," Brad replied. "I do believe that God is trustworthy."

"Would you like to ask him to take away from you these doubts that cling to your heart, making it hard for you to trust?"

"Yeah, I would," said Brad.

Brad bowed his head and said a simple prayer. He asked God to remove from him the lingering doubts that troubled him so much and that had, for so many years, made trusting hard. Then I decided to simply take a check and see if there was perhaps a way in which Jesus could be painted into this painful situation in Brad's life. As Brad concluded his prayer, I simply said softly, "Brad, when you think back to that experience, is there any scene that stands out in your mind—any way in which you picture that memory?"

Immediately Brad shot back, "Yes, there is. I was just coming home from school, and I stepped up onto the front porch. I heard something from inside, and I sat down there, outside of the screen door."

I continued, "And that's where you heard the bad news."

"Yes," he replied.

"Brad, I often find it helpful to simply picture God with us in our most painful memories—at our most difficult times. I actually picture *Jesus* there. I myself believe that Jesus *was* God's Son come to earth, so I picture him there with me. Would you like to try to picture God with you at that difficult time?"

"Yes, I think I would," he said.

I said a simple prayer, asking God to help Brad see him there as the One who was always faithful, always loving to Brad, and who could always be counted on and trusted.

"Brad, can picture him there?" I asked.

"Yes, I can," Brad replied.

I felt glad and relieved. "How do you see him?" I asked.

"I picture him hovering above me about thirty feet in the air," he said.

I thought to myself that it was interesting that Brad had pictured Jesus above him, watching over him.

"Brad, can you imagine, in your mind, Jesus floating down towards you and finally coming to rest right beside you—right next to you? He is beside you, and you're not looking at him, but he puts his arm around you and gives you a squeeze to let you know that he'll never leave you no matter *what* happens, to let you know that you can *always* trust him to be there to help you. Can you picture that?"

"Yes, I can," Brad replied.

"How does that make you feel?" I asked.

"Good . . . comforted," he said.

After a moment of silence, I spoke to Brad. "It's really neat to picture God with us in our difficult times, isn't it?"

"Yeah," he said. "I've never really thought of it like that before."

Seeing a look of deep wonder and amazement in Brad's eyes, I again asked him, "How does it feel to think of God there with you at that difficult time in your life?"

"It's really good. Like I'm really not alone in that thing."

"Yes," I replied. "He's always with us."

The Centrality of Jesus Christ

When I began my work as a spiritual counselor at the alcoholism treatment center, I was already an ordained pastor in the Lutheran Church. But I didn't know much about how to share my faith with other people. Oh, I knew what I believed! I could have written a wonderful summary of the Christian faith. I could preach sermons. I could have even taken people through a ten-week course on the basics of Christian doctrine. What I *didn't* know was how to communicate what I believed with people in a nonchurch setting. I didn't know how to listen for what other people believed, or how to dialogue with them in a way that made the saving work of God through Christ sensible to them in their current situation.

So for the first six months or so, all I did at the treatment center was to listen. People told me their whole life story and their defects of character, and I just listened. (I believe now this was a good place to start.) Then I began to dialogue more with people as I saw patterns emerge or heard something in one person's story that shed light on another's. After about a year and a half, the thought began coming to me that I should pray with people at the treatment center. So I began offering to pray for people after they had told me their fifth step. (I always proceed in spiritual matters only with people's permission.) And to my surprise, about 95 percent of the people accepted

44

my offer to pray for them. After some months of this, I began to ask people if *they* would like to pray at the end of their fifth step. About 30 to 40 percent of the people wanted to do that (the others still wanted me to pray for them). After doing this for some time, I began to think maybe we should stop and pray in the middle of our conversations when they had come to a particularly deep issue. This increased the intensity of people's prayers quite a bit. They went from "God, please bless me and help me stay sober" to "Oh, God, *please* help me to deal with this thing that has been bothering me for so many years!"

And it was about this point when I became acquainted with the idea of looking to see Jesus in our most painful moments. When I witnessed what a dramatic and healing effect this could have in people's lives, I was eager to offer this opportunity to people. But one thing quickly became apparent. This kind of prayer was of necessity Christ-centered. It rested firmly on the fact of God's incarnation in Christ because only in Christ could we ever *see* God. Everybody *prays* (there are no atheists in foxholes), but those who simply pray to their "Higher Power" cannot picture him. For the Creator can't be pictured. Only Jesus, the God who became Man, can be *pictured* with us in our suffering.

Some people were already familiar with Jesus and believed that he was the One God sent to earth to save us. But others were totally in the dark about Jesus. Either they were confused and conflicted about him or they knew virtually nothing about who he was.

When I realized this, I began to think seriously about my need to tell people about Jesus. Not as a sermon or a series of classes but in simple statements that made clear to people the Good News of who Jesus was and what he did for us. I had to learn not to be afraid or ashamed to speak of the Good News one-to-one, face-to-face, because it is the power of God to save everyone who believes. And how can they believe in the One of whom they have not heard?

So I began asking people if I could tell them what I believed about forgiveness or death or resentment or whatever they were struggling with. And then I would briefly explain the Good News of Jesus as it related to that topic. (Whenever possible, I would use the actual words of the Bible.) When people indicated that they believed the message, I would go on and offer them the opportunity to put their faith into action and pray for Jesus's help with their painful memories. And of course, wonderful things resulted!

ℰℭ

Kathy: Attempted Murder

I had worked with Kathy about a year previously, at which time, we prayed for Jesus to heal the memory of one of Kathy's childhood traumas. Kathy told me that since that time, the memory, which had previously driven her crazy, no longer bothered her. So she was eager to work on healing another traumatic memory.

"I've been having a lot of flashbacks lately," she said, "about the times when my husband tried to kill me. We're not living together now, but the memories still haunt me."

"Do you want to tell me what happened?" I asked.

"Well, it began with an argument. We were both drinking, and I started to say things that I knew would make him angry. That's the worse part about it," said Kathy." I feel like it's all my responsibility—that if I wouldn't have said the things I did, none of this would have happened."

"Now let's stop there for just a minute, Kathy," I said. "It may certainly be true that you were wrong in saying some of the things you did. But that doesn't excuse your husband for doing what *he* did. He still chose to get violent with you."

"I know," admitted Kathy. "Everybody keeps telling me the same thing—it's not my fault. But somehow, I can't believe it. I always felt that it was my responsibility to control my husband."

"Well," I replied, "you're being honest with me, and that's where we'll start. Let's go on."

"Well, our argument got heated, and then there came a time when the look on his face completely changed. I've talked to other women who have seen the same vacant stare of absolute rage on the face of a man. Then he began throwing me around the room, slamming me into walls. I remember thinking 'I'm going to die.' The only thing that saved me was that our teenage son Jake came running up the stairs with a hockey stick in his hand. He yelled repeatedly until he got my husband's attention, and that stopped the situation."

"OK," I said. "Shall we try to picture Jesus in that situation with you?" I asked. Kathy nodded and took my hands and bowed her head.

"Can you picture yourself in that memory now?" I asked. Kathy nodded.

"What do you see or feel?" I asked.

"I see myself being thrown into the wall and sliding down onto the carpet," Kathy replied.

When she said those words, I pictured Jesus catching Kathy in his arms as she fell to the floor.

"Can you picture Jesus catching you in his arms as you fall?" I asked.

"Yes, I can," said Kathy.

"How does that feel?" I asked.

"It feels soft and warm," replied Kathy.

"Does Jesus say any words to you?" I asked.

"No," replied Kathy. "He just holds me." Kathy let out a cry that came with tears of agony and almost sounded like a voice of a little girl.

"Why is he trying to kill me!" she said and repeated this over and over. I held Kathy's hand tightly as she suffered again through the agony of wondering why the one she loved the most was hurting her so badly. After the tears subsided somewhat, I asked Kathy, "How do you feel now?"

"I feel like I want to run away," replied Kathy.

I paused for a moment and then went on. "Can you picture yourself looking into the eyes of Jesus as if to say 'What do you want me to do now?'"

Kathy nodded.

"He tells me just to lie still, just to be still."

"Your husband is still in the room," I said. "What does Jesus do about that?"

Kathy paused for a moment and then said, "I see Jesus looking across at Jim, not with an angry look but a look of unconditional raw love that makes Jim fall to the floor crying."

As Kathy said that, a great uncontrollable sob rose up in me, and for a few moments, I simply cried deeply. I remember thinking, *Where in the world is* this *coming from? Am I identifying so deeply with Jim because I am also a man . . . or because I too have done things I sorely regret?* In any case, I had to cry for a moment.

Once the wave of emotion passed, I said to Kathy, "Can you picture Jesus holding up his hand to you as if to say 'Just stay here for a moment. I'll be right back'? And then Jesus goes over to Jim and touches him. Can you picture that, Kathy?" I asked.

"I picture Jesus holding Jim and rocking him like a baby," said Kathy.

"Is that a good place for the memory to end now?" I asked.

Kathy nodded.

Both Kathy and I took a moment to wipe away the tears and catch our breath. Then I commented to Kathy, "I think it's so interesting that as we invited Jesus to come into your heart and heal this memory, he not only appeared as the one to rescue *you* but the one to rescue Jim as well."

"I know!" replied Kathy. "I could never understand why someone who loved me would try to kill me. But I see now that Jim was in as much pain as I was. I actually heard and felt Jim's pain when you cried out as I described Jesus looking at Jim. And I feel the fear has been broken. When things like this happen . . . I can't explain it. It's like fear wraps me up like a mummy. I can't move forward or backward. But now, I honestly feel like Jesus has brought me out of that fear. And I see one more thing clearly as well. I see now that there's no way I could control Jim. Only Jesus's love is powerful enough to change Jim's behavior."

"I'm glad you see that more clearly now, Kathy. And I think we both understand that even though you can envision your husband responding to the love of Jesus, only *Jim* can actually take the step to make that happen. Only when he personally opens up and listens to the voice of Jesus and looks into those eyes of 'unconditional raw love,' as you described it, will he find the power to change in his actual experience."

"I know that's true," replied Kathy. "And I know I need to keep my hands off the matter and let Jesus work on changing my husband himself."

"That is certainly true, Kathy. But we *can* pray together and ask Jesus to help your husband respond to his love as we have seen it in this prayer time. Shall we pray together?"

"Yes, let's," she responded. Kathy prayed first, thanking Jesus for healing her and asking him to help her keep her hands off the situation as Jesus went to work to change her husband's heart. "Help me not to reach in and spoil things," she prayed.

Then I too prayed and asked God to change the heart of Kathy's husband and to enable him to respond to Jesus's love as we had envisioned it while praying together. When the prayer was done, Kathy said, "Thanks. I feel so much better."

I knew that there was much work ahead for Kathy. But I knew also that today, we had taken a big step in healing an important memory.

Note: As part of her healing process, Kathy entered a four-week inpatient treatment program for victims of domestic abuse.

80 08

Carl: Loneliness

Carl was a big man, and I thought him rather handsome as he sat down in my office. His hair was cut short on the top and it had grown long toward his shoulders and back. A stylish mustache wrapped around his chin and upper lip. But in spite of his big build, it soon became clear that he also had a tender heart. His eyes went misty, and a tear crept out the corner of his eye as he began talking to me about his program of recovery from alcoholism. He said he wanted to connect with God, but he wasn't sure that his prayers were being heard—that he was doing it right.

Carl described how his father and mother had parted early in his life, and his mother had moved in with a boyfriend who was unkind to him and his sister.

"He locked us in a room by ourselves and would take away our toys and laugh at us," Carl remembered.

We talked on, and after a few minutes, Carl again repeated the story about when he had been locked in a room. Having repeated it, almost unintentionally, it caught his attention. He commented how it was funny he would've written it down twice as he had been recording his thoughts. It made me wonder if it hadn't made a deeper impact on that young boy than even Carl himself realized. So I asked him, "Carl, can you still picture that scene of what happened when you were locked into a room alone?"

"Oh, yes," he said. "I can see it all—the house, the room."

"How did you feel?" I asked.

Carl thought for a moment. "Afraid," he said.

"And alone?" I suggested.

"Yes."

"Carl," I said, "I know that to you, it may seem like this was a small experience, but I think sometimes the sadness and the emotional pain that we carry with us in life are simply a collection of lots of little hurts, little disappointments, little experiences of fear. By themselves, they are not huge mountains. But like stones collected in a backpack on our shoulder, they weigh us down and cause our soul to be burdened with sadness."

Carl nodded understandingly.

"And so," I said, "the question is, How can we take a thing like this seemingly small experience from your past and take it out of the pack—take that stone off your back—and set it aside so you don't have to carry it anymore?

"I believe that God helps us do that," I continued, "simply by sharing with us the experiences we go through. I, for one, have often wished that God would prevent all the hurts and pains that we experience. And yet that's not the way life is. But what I am sure of, Carl, is that God wants to share our sorrows. You see, I believe Jesus, the man who lived two thousand years ago, actually was God walking on this planet. God coming into our mess, our world, and coming into our lives in such a way that he could carry the pains that we experience. And although he is not here now in a bodily way like he was two thousand years ago, he promised that in spirit, he would never leave us. He promised that his Spirit would be there to bring his comforting presence to us throughout all of the ages."

Carl nodded, showing that he was tracking with what I had said.

"Carl," I asked, "would you like to simply pray and ask God to share with you in that experience you had as a young boy?"

"I guess I would," said Carl. "But how would I do that?"

"It's pretty simple, really," I said. "I usually just ask God to help me picture him there with me in the time of my suffering. Would you like to give that a try?" I asked.

"OK," said Carl, shrugging as if to say "I'm game."

We joined hands and bowed heads. I said, "Carl, can you describe to me what you see as you think back to that memory?"

"I just see an empty room. I can't even really remember the face of the man who was my mom's boyfriend that locked us in."

As I listened to Carl, I thought that the real hurt to be healed was not a hatred toward the man whose face he had long ago forgotten but simply a healing of the fear and loneliness that being locked in a room had caused him.

"I wouldn't worry about remembering his face," I said. "Can you remember how you *felt* in that room?"

And again, Carl said, "Afraid, alone."

"Would you simply like to ask Jesus to be there with you?"

Carl said a simple prayer, asking Jesus to share that memory with him. I said, "Carl, can you picture him there with you now?" After a moment of silence, Carl said through tears, "Yes, I can see him."

"How do you picture it?" I asked.

"I see it like I've seen him in pictures. He looks like I've seen him in the pictures."

"Can you picture him reaching out and touching you—putting his arm around you?"

Carl's tears continued to flow as he affirmed that, yes, he could see Jesus with his arm around him, comforting him.

"How does it feel picturing Jesus there with you?" I asked.

"It feels good. It feels like, like the door is still locked, but it doesn't matter anymore."

We gripped each other's hands more tightly, and then after a brief moment of silence, both of us sat up and dried the tears from our eyes.

"Wow," said Carl. "I've prayed before, but that's the first time I have ever felt anything."

We talked on, and Carl's openness and honesty enabled us to touch matters of importance and deal with them in ways that were clear and helpful. When Carl said that he had been trying to pray but he wasn't sure he was doing it right, we looked at Psalm 62:8: "Trust in the Lord, O people. Pour out your heart to him."

Carl said, "So all you need to do is just be honest and pour out what's in your heart? That's simple!"

When Carl said that he had asked God to come into his life but he wasn't sure if God *had* come in, we looked at Revelation 3:20.

We read there how Jesus said "I stand at the door. If anyone hears my voice and opens to me, I will come in and eat with him."

Again, Carl was struck at the simple, clear answers that the scriptures gave to his questions. Then Carl said, "I want to be saved spiritually, but I really don't even know what that's all about—what's involved in that." We looked into Acts 17, where a jailer who was overcome with fear uttered the words "What must I do to be saved?" And the response of Paul, the follower of Jesus, came simple and clear: "Trust in the Lord Jesus and you will be saved."

"That's really good news," said Carl. "It's just a matter of trusting the Lord."

"Yes," I said. "That's why the Gospel got that name. *Gospel* is simply Greek for 'good news.'"

"Ah, I see," said Carl, chuckling. "So that's why the Bible Club that I went to when I was a little boy was called the Good News Club!"

As we wrapped up our time of talking together, Carl expressed his desire to help others with the things he had learned spiritually. I thought back over our conversation, and it occurred to me that time and again, we had done three simple things: talked, opened God's Word, and prayed.

"Carl," I said, "it occurs to me that if you want to help others, just think back to what we've done today. It began with you thinking about something important and opening up to me to talk it over. Secondly, we checked out what God had to say on the subject. Then, when we got to the heart of an important matter, we simply prayed about it. Thinking and talking, opening up to God, and praying. When you take the first letter of each of those, it's TOP—talk, open up to God, pray. You know, Carl, I think when we follow those simple steps, we'll stay on top of things spiritually."

Carl said, "Hey, that's cool! It's easy to remember. Can I write that down?"

"Sure." I nodded.

Buried

A while back, I was reading in 1 Corinthians 15 and noticed that Paul mentioned that he considered it of "first importance" (i.e., top priority) that Christ died, was buried, and that he rose on the third day. I could understand the importance of Christ's death and his resurrection, but what was so important about the fact that Christ was *buried*?

After praying and meditating on this question, I realized that many of the things that have affected us most deeply and have, in fact, hardwired us to react to situations the way we do are things that have been long buried as far as our conscious mind. Often these events happened early in our childhood and had immense impact on our young, delicate emotions. Often they formed convictions in us about how life and relationships with other people were to function. And of course, often these convictions and vows that we may have subtly made were based on lies that were incredibly wide of the truth. Yet they became our operating procedures. And though the events in which these beliefs were formed have been long forgotten, the emotional and behavioral responses continue.

Then I realized, *this* is the reason that it was of first importance that Jesus was buried! Because he was buried, he is able to go with us into the graves of our experiences to the places where some of our most important memories have been buried.

And from there, he is able to lead us out into the light of day, having breathed new life and truth into our experiences.

In the following story, Jesus worked with a friend of mine to dust off memories that were long buried but which held the key to helping him understand why he was stuck in sinful patterns and how he could change his behaviors for the better.

ഓരു

Ray: Violent Reactions

Ray was a Native American man in his forties who had spent about half his adult life in prison (he was known as one of the toughest fighters in town). But during his last incarceration, he had become a believer in Jesus. When I stopped in to see Ray one day, he was pretty jazzed about something that had happened.

"You know, I've been thinking lately about how it's my default setting to react with violence anytime I feel someone is threatening or disrespecting me or one of my friends or family. I don't stop to listen or try to understand. I just go right to fight mode! And I started to ask myself why I do that. I really didn't have any idea, so I asked Jesus, 'Jesus, why do I do that? Why do I always go right to fighting?'

"Almost instantly, I'm going back in my mind to a little house we lived in when I was just a boy. My dad had built a kind of attic space, but when I climbed up there on the ladder, I stepped in the wrong place and my foot went through the ceiling. My dad came over and pulled me out of the attic and threw me onto the floor. It was pretty bad. He really lost it and was kicking and punching me. I thought he was maybe gonna kill me! And my mother was there too, off to the side, but she was just laughing. Well, that's the scene that I went back to.

"But this time, it was like Jesus had me tucked under his arm and was pointing things out to me. First, I realized that my dad was actually mad at *himself* for making the ceiling too weak. But he didn't know any other way to deal with his anger, so he just took it out on me. Just seeing that was a kind of healing right there. Then I realized that my mother was laughing, but she wasn't laughing *at* me, she was afraid too—hysterical, really. And she knew that if she tried to stop him, he would turn on her too. So again, that was the only thing she felt she could do. And that was another healing for me.

"But then, the real kicker came. Jesus said to me—and this one was so clear, it was almost like a voice I could hear—'You're fighting to try to save *him*.'

"And suddenly, I could see it all! When I was lying there on the floor, trying to shield myself from the blows, I remember thinking, 'Nobody is coming to save me!' And after that, whenever I flew into a rage to protect one of my friends or family, I wasn't really fighting to save them, *I was fighting to save myself!* I was trying to save that little boy who had no one to save him. And now it was like Jesus was looking calmly at me and saying, 'You want to know why you fight? *That's* why you fight.'"

"Wow," I said, "that's amazing. I never would have guessed it, but it makes perfect sense. Does the memory still feel hurtful, or does it feel better now? I mean, is God there now?"

"I thought about that, and yes, he is there. See, I noticed as I was looking at that memory this time that there was a bright beam of light shining down on that scene where all this happened. And there was no window in that old house to let light in like that, so I know that's actually the presence of God with me. That was always the worst part about it—I felt like I was all alone." Then Ray leaned toward me just slightly and said in a low, serious voice, "But I wasn't really alone—he *was* with me."

৯০ ୯ଓ

56

Robert: Accidental Death

I had known Robert for about four or five weeks before talking with him extensively, and I had liked him from the start. He was a friendly man, about thirty-five years old with a clean-cut look. But there was a jitteriness about him that made me think there was some sort of fear inside of Robert. I also felt a kind of hollowness in his life that I couldn't quite explain.

When we began talking, he told me about his childhood— how he had grown up with a very oppressive father. His father took the family to church on a regular basis but also drank heavily and, when drunk, would come home and make threats. Robert related a time when his father came home drunk, put a gun to his own head in front of Robert, and said, "I think I'll just do you a favor and kill myself." I couldn't imagine the terror that such an experience would have put into a young boy.

We talked on, and Robert referred to an episode that happened on his eighteenth birthday. Because he was then legally able to buy liquor, he and two friends had gotten some booze and gone out joyriding. They were driving around that night when all of a sudden, they struck two young people who were walking on the road. Robert found out later that both of the young people, a pair of boys age twelve and sixteen, had been killed. I thought what a deep sorrow that event would have left in Robert's life. But I far underestimated how deeply it had affected him. We talked on, and he continued relating his experiences to me. We got to the topic of Robert's relationship with God, and I asked him where he was with God.

Robert replied, "I want to know God personally, but I know that I don't. I've been reading the Bible lately, figuring that maybe I can meet him there."

I remember thinking to myself that Robert was certainly on track; the Bible is a good place to meet God. But it takes more than simply reading the words of the Bible. It takes interacting with the God of the Bible—bringing to him our sins for his forgiveness, depending on his gifts of hope and life for our security. I wondered to myself how I could help Robert experience for himself all the gifts that God had for him.

We talked on, and Robert related an incident that had happened in the recent past when he had a violent outburst against his wife and swung at her with intent to kill her. Only because his hand had struck an object before it hit her had he not succeeded. He felt a terrible load of guilt over his evil intent to hurt his wife. We talked together about the forgiving nature of God. I shared with Robert my faith that God actually became one of us humans in the person of Jesus of Nazareth. In his death on the cross, Jesus suffered the sins of the whole world so that he might, with God's authority, truly forgive us for the wrongs we've done. I asked Robert if he wanted to pray and tell God he was sorry for what he had done to his wife, and Robert said yes.

We bowed our heads, and Robert spoke a brief but heartfelt prayer, asking God's forgiveness for what he had done to his wife. Then somehow, I sensed that it was time for us to revisit the experience that Robert had had on his eighteenth birthday, when his joyriding had caused the accidental death of two boys.

"Robert," I asked, "can you still remember what happened that night when those boys were killed? Can you still picture it in your mind?"

"Yes," Robert answered. "I remember I was in the car with my two friends. One of them, the older one, was driving. And the other one and I were riding. I remember a thud and a clank as we hit something and it rolled over the top of the car. But we didn't stop or look back. We just kept driving. I had this sick feeling, wondering what we had done. Some days later, the police caught up to us and showed me pictures of the two boys as they lay in the ditch after they had been hit by our car. They were twisted in all kinds of unnatural ways. Their bones and limbs were broken, and one boy's face was all bloody on one side. They looked like Raggedy Ann dolls when you throw them down, and they end up all twisted in a knot."

Now I faced a dilemma. I wanted Robert to receive God's healing for this tragedy. I wanted him to picture Jesus there with them that night. And yet his own memory was split into two parts—the accident itself and the pictures he saw of the boys after the accident had happened. So I asked Robert if he could, on the basis of what he saw in the pictures, imagine himself there in the ditch with those boys on the night when the accident happened.

"Yes, I can," Robert said.

"Robert," I said, "have you ever read that 'Footprints' poem—the one about Jesus being there with us in our darkest times when we thought he had abandoned us?"

"Yeah, I've read it," Robert said.

"Would you like to picture Jesus there with you on that horrible night when those boys were killed?"

"I would," said Robert.

And so we prayed and asked God to help Robert picture Jesus there. Then I asked Robert where Jesus would be in his memory. "Can you see him there in the ditch with you that night?"

"Yes, I can," Robert replied.

"Where is he?" I asked.

"I see him standing on the other side of the two boys."

"What does he look like?" I asked.

"He's all dressed in white."

"Does he say anything to you?" I asked. "Or does he make any gestures at all to you?"

Robert thought for a moment, his eyes closed, and then he said, "He just simply lifts his hand toward me."

In my own mind, I thought how important it would be for Robert to see Jesus connecting with him that night, so I asked, "Can you picture yourself reaching out and taking Jesus's hand?"

After another short pause, Robert replied, "I can picture myself reaching out to him."

"Can you picture Jesus taking hold of *your* hand?" I said.

"Yes, I can," Robert replied.

"Can you picture him drawing you into his arms and hugging you to himself right there?"

Robert was crying now. He nodded. I asked Robert how it felt to be in Jesus's embrace.

He replied, "Like it's going to be OK . . . like everything is going to be OK."

After a moment of simply soaking up the divine love, I said to Robert, "Those boys left this world and went into God's eternal realm that night. What do you picture Jesus doing about those two boys?"

"I picture those boys leaving with Jesus," Robert said.

"Do they somehow stand up and go to Jesus?" I asked.

"No, they just disappear. They just vanish along with Jesus," Robert replied.

"So now in your memory, you're left there by yourself," I said.

"That's right," Robert said. "But it's OK! I feel OK now. As a matter of fact, I feel life isn't hopeless anymore. Always before, I felt like everything that happened after that night was worthless—my whole life was a mockery after that. Whatever I did was in vain."

"How do you feel now?" I said to Robert.

"I feel like . . . when you come home after you've been gone a long time and everybody's glad to see you and everyone makes a big fuss about you. I feel like that. I feel like I'm home."

He looked up at me, and he said, "You know, I always feared that God could never forgive me for what took place that night. But I know now that he has. Always before, whenever I would even talk about God, I would get this tight feeling in my stomach. But it's not there anymore."

About a week later, I talked again to Robert and asked him how he felt after our conversation and prayer to God about his difficult memories and painful experiences in the past.

"I still feel good," Robert said. "For one thing, I feel like a *person* again. To tell you the truth, I often felt like I was a walking dead man before we talked and prayed about this. But now, I feel like a whole person again. I feel at peace. And now when I talk to God and pray, I don't have the fear anymore."

"The fear?" I asked.

"Yeah. Before, whenever I would pray or even think about God, I'd get this tight fear in my stomach. But it's gone! I don't feel it anymore! I know I have to stay in touch with God and stay close to him. But now I feel at peace in his presence. Now I *want* to be with him!"

Note: Some months later, I was talking with another man at the treatment center. He had been in the program previously with Robert. Without my prompting, he mentioned the change he had noticed in Robert. "When I saw him after he did his fifth step with you, he looked like a different man! He looked so peaceful. I noticed it right away when I saw him that day. He had never been able to sit still—always pacing and jittery. But he was just sitting there, so calm. His face was just about glowing!"

Grandma Loretta:
Negative Childhood Prophesies

Grandma Loretta looked entirely the part of loving grandmother as she came into my office to talk with me. Her eyes sparkled from behind gold-rimmed glasses, and her smile was genuine and bright. She told me how good she felt to be recovering from her addiction to alcohol.

"I had a really hard time after my husband died," Loretta admitted. "He was like a Rock of Gibraltar to me. He used to take care of everything around the house. We went to Bible study together . . . Although in our later years, that kind of dropped off. After he passed away, I really began drinking heavily. Truth of the matter is, I've never been on my own in life before. At first, there were my parents, then my husband, Roger. This is the first time I've ever been alone and . . . I think I'm scared."

I invited Loretta to tell me more about herself. She began with her childhood. She talked about several of her childhood memories, then hit on one that struck me as unusual and important.

"I remember going to visit my uncle Myron when I was a little girl. I was a very petite child, and Myron would always bounce me on one knee. And every time, he would say the same thing. He would put me on his knee facing away from him, bounce me up and down, and say, 'Is Loretta ever going to amount to anything?' And then he would turn me around to face him, look at me, and say, 'Nope, I don't think she's ever going to amount to anything!' I think he did it kind of as a joke to be funny, but oh, how I hated it! All through my elementary school years and then my high school years, I always had that fear in my mind that I would never amount to anything. Now that I think of it, that's probably why I'm so scared now that Roger is dead. Now I'm on my own and 'Is Loretta ever going to amount to anything?'" Her voice caught.

"Loretta, your uncle really hurt you by what he said, didn't he?" I observed.

Loretta nodded.

"You know it's almost funny how that experience was just a simple little thing, but it has really had a deep and long-lasting impact in your life, hasn't it?"

"It really has!"

"Loretta," I continued, "do you think your uncle understood how much what he said would hurt you and trouble you over the years?"

"No, I don't think so. I *know* he didn't."

"I don't think so either. But even though he didn't understand it, he did hurt you pretty deeply. He planted fear in your life based on the lie that you had to *do* something to make your life worthwhile. You had to amount to something. But what is God's truth? Isn't it that you are worthy and your life amounts to something simply because he loves you?"

"I think so. I never really thought of it like that. But it makes a lot of sense, doesn't it?" responded Loretta.

"Loretta, would you like to take a minute and pray and simply tell God you forgive your uncle for the things he said that hurt you so deeply?"

"Yes, I would."

"May I join hands with you while we pray?"

"Sure."

"Go ahead and say whatever you want to God."

"Dear Lord," Loretta prayed, "please forgive Uncle Myron for what he said to me when I was a little girl. I know he didn't realize what he was doing to me, and I forgive him. Please help me recover and go on now by myself. I know I'm not really by myself because you're here with me. I thank you for that. In Jesus's name, amen."

Before I said anything in prayer, I thought of how good it would be to welcome Jesus into Loretta's painful memory. Keeping my head bowed, I asked, "Loretta, can you still picture that scene in your mind when your uncle was bouncing you on his knee?"

"Yes, I can."

"Would you like to invite Jesus to be part of that picture?"

"Yes, I would. And I can see him there now."

"How do you see it?"

"Jesus is right there with us. He has his arm around both me and Uncle Myron."

"How does it feel?"

"Better. Much better."

The Real Problem: Believing a Lie

At the heart of every wounded person is a lie. It might be "I'm not worth anything, and nobody loves me." It might be "What's the use of trying? I'll only fail anyway." It might be "You can't trust anybody!" Or it might be one of a few hundred other variations of Satan's deceptions. And those lies are what really cripple us.

Usually, we are not consciously aware of the lies we believe. We are simply aware of how they make us feel: worthless, depressed, anxious, afraid, ashamed, dirty, etc. And often, these lies have their roots back in our childhood, when our hearts were tender and most susceptible to being wounded. A boy who is beaten by his father may have bruises that will last a couple of days. But the lies that he may come to believe can wound him for years—literally *all his life* unless God's truth intervenes.

I sometimes think of the wound as a cut on the arm and the lie as the infection that Satan tried to get into that cut. As everyone knows, a little cut on our arm can't really hurt us seriously. But if infection sets in, we could end up losing the whole arm or even our life! So the wounds we suffer in childhood provide an "opening." And Satan tries to rub "dirt" into the wound and infect us with a lie. For he knows that if he can get us to believe his lies, it will prove deadly to our spiritual life.

When we go back to pray about painful episodes from the past, sometimes God will communicate a verbal message, such as "This was not your fault" or "Things are going to be OK." These messages are, of course, to counteract the lies that were implanted in a person's mind when they were traumatized and vulnerable to Satan's lies. Often, it seems God works according to the old saying "A picture is worth a thousand words." For a woman who has been sexually abused, to see a mental picture of Jesus present and embracing her after her abuse can be a powerful, lie-busting statement that she is *not* dirty. She is *not* unlovable. She is *not* irreparably broken. But in fact, she is loved by the most important person of all.

Whether communicated through words or in pictures, Jesus is the Truth that will set us free.

⃝⃞

Grant: Stillborn Brother

Grant's jet-black hair exemplified his Native American heritage as he seated himself in my office to take his fifth step in the process of recovery from alcoholism. He told about his family background (mom and dad and one sister) and his current family situation (married with one young daughter). After covering a few more topics, I queried, "What about your spiritual life? What do you believe about God?"

"I don't know," answered Grant honestly. "I know where my dad is at with God. But I don't know about myself. I really wish I could get back to being close with God."

"You say 'get back' with God. Was there a time in your past when you felt you *were* close to God?"

"Yes, but it was a long time ago."

"How long ago?"

"When I was really young. Like about three or four. I can remember how I actually *felt* God was with me!"

"What happened to change that?" I asked.

"My brother died."

"I'm sorry," I said. "Would you like to tell me about how he died?"

"Well, he was stillborn, actually. I remember my mother being pregnant. She told me I was going to have a little brother or sister. Man, was I excited! I used to talk to my brother when he was still inside my mother. But he died at birth. I can still remember holding him!"

"Can you picture that scene in your mind still today?"

"Oh, yes."

"What do you see?"

"I see myself holding my little brother and crying. And my mom and dad are next to each other in front of me."

"And that's when your heart turned away from God?"

"Yup. I can remember it was like a wall went up between me and God. I thought, 'How could God ever do something like this!' From that day on, whenever I went to church—and my parents took me to church a couple times a week—I had my guard up against God. I wasn't going to let him in my life! I actually went the other way and got involved in, like, occult things. And drugs and alcohol . . . lots of that."

"You know, Grant," I began, "I know it's very commonplace to blame God for things like what happened to your brother. But I don't think God wanted that to happen any more than you did. Think of it—when God created the world, there was no such thing as death. That only came about when people began to disobey God and sin entered the world. In fact, I think your brother's death hurt God as much or even *more* than it hurt you! That's what I believe the cross was all about—God suffering the effects of sin in the world, one of which was a little Indian boy who died at birth and left a big brother who was heartbroken. Does that make any sense, Grant?"

"Yes, it does. I've never looked at it that way before."

"As a matter of fact, I think you can look at it two ways, both equally true. You can look at the pain that you felt that day as being part of the pain Jesus suffered on the cross the day he died. Or you can flip it around and say that Jesus's suffering on the cross meant that he was there with you the day your brother died. He was there hurting right alongside you and your parents."

"That's a really different way to look at it!" admitted Grant.

"Grant, would you like to pray with me and ask Jesus to heal the wound that you suffered the day your brother died? Maybe to ask him help you see him there with you?"

"Yes, I would," replied Grant.

We joined hands, and I said, "Go ahead . . . however you'd like to say it to God."

Grant prayed, "Lord, I'm sorry for turning my heart away from you the day my brother died. I know now that you weren't the reason for that. Please heal me . . . heal the wound in my heart. And let me be close to you again. In Jesus's name, amen."

"Grant," I said softly, my eyes still closed. "You know how you said you could still picture the day your brother died? Can you see that scene in your mind?"

"Yes."

"Can you see Jesus there with you now?"

"Yes, I can."

"Where is he? How does he look?"

"He's got a white robe and long brown hair. He's standing behind my parents with one hand on each of their shoulders. And he's looking right at me."

"How does it feel to have him there?"

"Good. It feels peaceful. Like I know I can trust God again now."

Note: Grant went on to make an excellent step of recovery from alcoholism and to reconnect with God, becoming a member of a church in his area.

ഇൗ

Josh: Childhood Sexual Abuse

I felt somewhat intimidated by Josh when he first stepped into my office. He was a big boy! He was about twenty years old, stood above six feet, and must have weighed in over 260 pounds. His hair was clipped short and frosted at the tips—very hip!

Josh began telling me about his background. Father left when he was two. Mother was an alcoholic. Then he touched a tender nerve. "When I was about five, one of my mother's boyfriends molested me."

"Have you ever had a chance to talk about this experience with anyone?" I asked.

"I mentioned it in my small group here at the treatment center. I cried when I talked about it, but it felt good to get it out. That was the first time I told anyone about it. No, wait. I did tell my mother back when I was a kid. But she just slapped me and told me to shut up. So I never told anybody after that. I don't know. I guess I'm not sure what to do with that experience."

I had been learning some things about the path of healing for sexual abuse, so I laid it out for Josh as clearly as I could. "Josh, I believe there are three steps toward healing for something like what you've gone through. The first is to find a place where you feel free enough to tell the story of what happened. I don't mean just saying you were sexually abused. I mean feeling safe enough to actually tell what you remember—what happened and how it made you feel. The second step is to recognize what effect that experience has had on you—how it has changed the way you look at yourself and the world. The third step is to forgive the person who did that to you. That may seem like an impossibility for you at the moment. But if you take the first two steps, it may appear much more reasonable. It's kind of like if you asked me to jump across this room, I would think that impossible for me. But if you said I could take it in three leaps, well, I could get one-third of the way with each jump. And I think I could do that."

"So what you want me to do . . . like, tell what he actually did to me?" posed Josh.

"I don't *want* you to do anything. You do what you want to do. I just wanted to give you what I've seen to be the pathway for healing from something like this. And if you *want* to talk about it, that's fine. We've got the time."

Josh paused for a moment. (He told me later he seriously considered not saying anything and just about moved on to another topic.) "Well, he used to have me come in and watch porn movies with him." Josh went on to tell me about the rough outlines of the sexual abuse that took place."

"How did that stuff leave you feeling?" I asked.

"Afraid."

"I know *I* would have been afraid if I had been in your shoes."

"And I remember being mad at God," Josh admitted.

"Good," I replied. "You're already at the second step—realizing how this experience has affected you."

"I guess I am!" Josh said with satisfaction. "Yeah, I went to a Catholic school, but this anger at God over what happened was always a block for me."

I thought we'd better try to deal with that anger. "Josh, I think many people sort of picture God as high above us in some kind of soundproof booth, pulling the levers and pushing the buttons that control things down here."

"Yeah, I guess I've kind of thought of him more or less like that."

"And we ask why God lets things happen like what happened to you. Why doesn't he stop it?"

"Yeah!"

"But have you ever stopped to ask *how* he could stop such things? I mean, do we want him to sort of freeze a man who is headed for a horrible act—like hitting pause on a video player? But then we have to decide who should be frozen. Just all the murderers and rapists? How about the men who come home drunk and yell at their kids? How about the women who go out on their husbands? Or the gang of kids who pick on the little boy down the block? Do you see, Josh, that if God did it that way, it wouldn't be long before the whole world was frozen?"

"Yeah. I guess I asked why he ever sent people like that into the world."

"That's a variation on the freezing idea, isn't it? But if God wanted to take all the evil people out of the world, again, where would he draw the line? If he really wanted to rid the world of evil, wouldn't he get rid of all of us?"

"I see what you mean."

"Josh, I believe God had a different plan. In Jesus, he got right into the middle of our mess. He became vulnerable. He exposed *himself* to the hurt. He suffered *with* us. He suffered all the wrong things that have ever been done in this world. And that brings us to the third step—forgiveness."

"Yeah, that's the hard one," admitted Josh.

"It may help to realize that God sees the whole picture. I mean, have you ever asked yourself who messed with your abuser?"

"You mean who molested him?"

"Yep."

"Do you think there was someone . . . when *he* was a little boy?"

"Nothing is more common! Now of course, I don't know. But the point is, *God* knows. He sees the hurt *behind* the wrong this man did to you. Jesus suffered it all! But he never let it turn to hate in his heart. He suffered that man's sins, but he forgives him. And I believe Jesus wants to help you forgive so this hurt doesn't become hate in *your* heart. I mean, who will that hurt? Your abuser?"

"No, *me*."

"Who else?" I ventured.

"My son."

"I'm glad you see that."

"You know, my son is seven months old now, and when I bathe him, I'm uncomfortable."

"And as long as you're tied to that experience, there will always be a part of you that's nervous and uncomfortable around your son. And deep inside, your son will ask, 'Why is there this uncomfortable feeling between Dad and me? Is it me?' But when you forgive your abuser, you say, 'Lord, I don't want to focus on him and on resenting him anymore. I want to let go of that and put him into your hands so I can turn my attention to the future—growing a warm, close, healthy relationship with my son.' Do you feel ready for that?"

"Amazingly, yes, I do."

We joined hands, and Josh prayed, "Lord, I want you to know that I forgive that guy for doing wrong to me. And I forgive *you*, Lord. I realize now that you really weren't approving of it or deserting me like I thought you were. Help me let go of this so I can be a good father to my son. Amen."

I felt so glad that Josh had taken the third step and had forgiven his abuser. "Josh," I said, "I often find help with painful memories by just picturing Jesus there with me. Would you like to try that?"

"Yes, I would," Josh replied.

"Is there a scene that sticks in your mind when you think back to the abuse?"

"Yes, there is. I'm in my bedroom on my bed, crying. I'm under the covers curled up in a fetal position."

I felt sad when I pictured this memory—a wound that had been hurting for years. "Can you picture Jesus standing at the door of your bedroom?"

"Yes."

"How do you see him? How does he look to you?"

"He has long brown hair and a beard and a white robe thing with a rope around his waist and sandals."

"Josh, can you picture Jesus coming in and sitting on your bed?"

"Yes, I can."

"Can you imagine him softly stroking your hair . . . then taking you in his arms and holding you?"

"Yes."

"And how does that feel?"

"A lot better!"

After a brief silence, we said "Amen."

"Wow," said Josh. "Before, when I thought of that scene, even just now, I could hardly breathe. With Jesus there, I could relax and breathe again."

Not Every Time

I would be telling less than the whole truth if I didn't admit that I'm not able to help every person I counsel to have a healing encounter with Jesus. There are many people I talk to (at the treatment center and in my daily life as a missionary to Native American people) with whom I don't get anywhere close to such a deep conversation. Many people are simply not ready to be that open with me. And I'm committed to not barging into people's lives like a bull in a china shop. It is my constant prayer that God will give me sharp eyes to not miss a single open door that he puts before me (even if it's only open a crack). But I also pray that he will give me the patience and faith so that I don't try to bust through a single locked door (thereby causing the person behind the door to simply retreat deeper into hiding).

So when I'm listening to a person, if I don't spot such an opening for the Good News of Jesus, I keep my mouth shut. Of course, I pray constantly for such openings (and the boldness to go through them), but even with that, I don't always find one.

And there are a few times when people surface a painful memory and we pray, but they can't seem to see Jesus there or receive much peace from him. I don't know why. And the last thing I want to do is make them feel like they've somehow failed. They've brought out their pain, and we've taken it to the Lord in prayer. From then on, it's in *his* hands. While God's promise of forgiveness and life in Christ are *always* sure, his response to our individual prayers for healing will probably always remain somewhat of a mystery. But we know that God wants to heal us and that he wants us to pray for his will to be done on earth as it is done in heaven.

In the following two stories, you will meet George and Joe. George couldn't see the living Christ in his painful memory, but he did have another odd experience that seemed to open him up to God's truth from scripture. Joe pictured Jesus in his memory but in a very static way that didn't seem to help him much.

I share these stories so that we will remember not to lose heart when our prayers are not answered in the way we might hope or expect. But I want to say again that what continues to amaze me is not the number of people who do *not* experience the presence and peace of Christ when we pray about painful experiences, but the vast number of people who *do*.

ॐ ⟨⟩

George: Stealing from a Church

George was about forty years old and recovering from drug addiction when I talked to him at the treatment center. He was kind of a rough-cut man, and he had several fingers cut off halfway on one hand (something that would prove significant later on). He told me that one of his motivations for getting sober was dealing with his guilt.

"There's one thing I did that really bothers me," he admitted. His eyes began to tear up as he struggled to get his words out. "I stole from a church when I was about thirteen! My dad always used to take me to a church when I was young, but I never went back after that! I won't even go into a church for a funeral or wedding now. I feel real bad about this one."

"Can you pinpoint how you feel?" I asked.

"Scared," he replied.

"Scared of God's anger or punishment over what you've done?"

"Yes. I've never been able to talk about this, although I mentioned it to my small group here in treatment. I just feel so bad about it!"

"Have you ever asked God to forgive you?"

"No."

"Would you like to? We could take a break and pray so you could tell God you're sorry for what you did and ask him to forgive you," I offered.

"I'd like to do that," George replied. We bowed our heads and joined hands as George prayed, "Lord, I'm sorry for what I did, stealing that money . . . Please forgive me." More tears came as George prayed his confession.

After a moment, I said, "Would you like to know what I believe that helps me in situations like this?"

"Yes, I would," replied George.

"First, I believe that we've *all* sinned—that every one of us has broken God's laws. I mean if you just run down the Ten Commandments, how do we stack up? You've already told me about stealing. How about 'Thou shalt not lie'? Ever done that?"

"Yes," responded George.

"Me too. Ever covet or envy what others have?"

"Yeah, I've done that."

"So have I. And it goes right on down the same way with dishonoring parents or using God's name disrespectfully or any of his other commands. We break them! But I believe a second thing—that God did something to save us. Jesus, who was both God and man, died with all our sins in his body on the cross as a ransom payment. Now a ransom payment allows somebody to go free, and we *all* were captives to our guilt. But he paid the fine so that we could go free!"

George grew wide-eyed. "I wish I'd have known this a long time ago!"

"Yeah, and there's more! After Jesus died and rose again to life, he ascended to heaven to give us the gift of the Holy Spirit. That way, God could be with us always and help us not to fall into the same mistakes."

Again, George spoke about the pain over what he had done.

"Would you like to pray and ask God to heal you from the hurt you brought on yourself?" I asked.

"Yes, I would . . . But I couldn't find the words!"

"Would you like me to pray for you?" I offered.

"Yes, if you would, please," replied George.

"Lord," I asked, "would you please heal George inwardly from the hurt he has experienced for so long over the wrong he did, stealing that money from a church?" Then I said, "George, can you picture Jesus with you in that church?"

George was quiet for a moment and then said, "There was a crucifix in the church when I stole that money."

"How does that make you feel?" I asked.

"Terrible," replied George.

I prayed again, "Lord, would you bring George your truth about what he did?" Then I asked again, "George, does anything else come to mind?"

"No."

I released George's hands, raised my head, and opened my eyes.

"That feels a little better," said George. Then he began rubbing his cut off fingers. "That's strange," he said. "I can feel my fingers! I've never had feeling in the ends of these fingers, but now"—he kept rubbing his fingers and turning his hands over—"that's amazing!"

"Does it feel like some kind of sign?" I asked.

"Yes, it does!"

"And what does the sign say?"

"That God forgives me? At least, I hope he does!"

"George, do you want to see a verse from scripture about forgiveness?" I asked.

"Yes."

I opened to 1 John 1:7 and read, "If we walk in the light . . . the blood of Jesus, his Son, purifies us from every sin . . . If we confess our sins, he is faithful and . . . will forgive us."

George exclaimed, "Is that in every Bible?"

"Yes, it is," I assured him.

"That's great! I really do feel like a load has been lifted off me. And my fingers . . . I can't believe it! I used to think that maybe God might answer prayers, but today, I *know* he does!"

Joe: Abusive Father

Joe was a big man in his midthirties. He was a chef by trade, and I met him in treatment, recovering from drug addiction. He explained how his life went during his childhood.

"I used to play with my friends until about ten p.m. Then my dad would take me along with him to the bar where I would sit in the car until midnight or one o'clock. It didn't matter if it was ninety degrees above or twenty below. I sat in that car. Then my father would finally come out, and I would drive home with my drunken father. I always feared dying in a car accident. When we got home, I would listen to my parents fight until about two o'clock. After that, it would take me a while to relax and fall asleep, and then I would have to get myself up to go to school. Needless to say, I was always tired and did poorly in school. As time went on, I pulled away from any friendships. Throughout my life, I've sabotaged those who got too close to me." Joe seemed to slump into a pause.

"Joe, may I ask you what you believe about God?"

"Well, I grew up a Lutheran. And my wife was Jehovah's Witness. I always had trouble with the idea of the Trinity, and then somebody explained it to me. It's kind of like water that can be three different forms: water, air, and ice."

"Have you ever forgiven your father for what he did when you were young?"

"No."

"Can I tell you what I believe about forgiveness?" I asked.

"Sure."

"Well, I believe we need power to forgive—kind of like a gas pedal is needed to make a car go. And I believe that power comes from Jesus who died on the cross for all our sins and who prayed, 'Father, forgive them, for they don't know what they're doing.' And then we need something to guide the process, like a steering wheel. And I believe that guidance is a three-step process of telling the story, identifying the effects of the wrong, and offering forgiveness. You've told me the story of what your father did. And you've done a good job identifying the effects—how it's caused you to pull away from people all through your life. Now would you like to take the step of telling God you forgive your father?"

"Sure," said Joe. We joined hands, and Joe prayed, "Jehovah, God, you know what happened with my father. I want to forgive . . . Please help me. Amen."

Still holding Joe's hands, I looked up and said to him, "Joe, I believe there's also an added step of asking God to *heal* us of the effects of the wrongs done to us. Would you like me to pray that God would heal you?"

"Sure."

I prayed for God to heal Joe and then asked, "Joe, can you picture Jesus there?"

"I can," replied Joe.

"How do you see him?"

"Like a statue on the back dashboard of the car."

"Does he communicate anything to you?"

"No."

"How does it feel as you look at the memory now?"

"I really don't feel anything."

Joe didn't seem to have gotten much relief or peace, but I couldn't think of anything more to say. And our conversations ended on other subjects.

Joleen: Premarital Sex

Joleen impressed me with her bright smile as we walked together into my office. She was about thirty-eight years old and dressed in wind pants and a sports jersey. She wore black combat boots, and her eyes were slightly hidden behind small oval glasses. All in all, she struck me as an interesting mix of a person.

We got to talking, and Joleen introduced herself, giving me a brief description of her childhood. It was not very happy.

"I had a hard time feeling like I belonged anywhere," stated Jo. "My dad was a hard worker—one of those people who thought that hard work would solve every problem. He was very authoritarian. His way was the only way, and everybody should see it! My mom was a weak person . . . still is to this day. I kind of despised her."

Jo continued, telling me about her brothers and sisters and then gave this summary statement: "I think I felt kind of lost as a child. Honestly, I still feel very lost. I don't really know where I belong."

"You know, Joleen," I responded, "I believe that a sense of belonging is one of the three most important emotional needs that every person has."

"How does a person get that?" posed Jo. Then she answered her own question. "I know, I have to find it inside me."

"Well, I might see that a little differently. I know it's very popular nowadays to say we have everything we need inside of us. But I believe that acceptance is something that we can only get from *someone else*. It's a gift that's *given* to us. Ultimately, I believe our deepest and most lasting sense of acceptance and belonging comes from our Maker. He created us, and we *belong* with him."

"I guess I believe that too," replied Jo. "I know there was one point in my life a few years ago when I made friends with a number of people from a certain church. I went with them to church for about a year, and I felt more like I belonged there than I'd ever felt anywhere else before."

"What made you stop going?" I asked.

"Well, I was hiding my drug use from them. And I never felt I could be open with them about all the bad things I'd done."

"So you began to live a double life."

"That's right. After a while, I just couldn't take it anymore and quit going."

Our conversation moved on, and Jo described her transition to adulthood. "I got interested in boys, and I guess I developed a reputation as a flirt, although I had never had sex with anyone. Not until I met Larry. I was seventeen, and I actually had another boyfriend at the time—Bill. But Larry was older and gave me lots of attention. He persuaded me to have sex with him, and shortly after that, he lost interest in me. I was crushed and kind of chased after him to try and get him back. But he treated me real badly. He said nasty things about me right to my face. I think he only let me hang around him so he could have sex with me. After a couple months, even that ended. That was a real turning point in my life. Things kind of went downhill from there. I let men do pretty much whatever they wanted with me. Then I got married. I'm just now in the process of getting a divorce after being in an abusive relationship with my husband for thirteen years."

"He would hit you?" I asked.

"Yeah. And I would let him," Jo stated flatly, sounding somewhat disgusted with herself.

Our conversation moved on to Jo's dreams and experiences vocationally. But her statement about the big turning point in her life stuck in my mind, and I couldn't listen very well to what she was now saying. So I interrupted, "Jo, could we go back a step or two? My mind is kind of stuck on what you said about how your life took a big turn there when you were seventeen."

"Oh, sure," agreed Jo. "It really was a turning point for me. I mean before that, I had felt kind of OK about myself. Like I said, things weren't that great at home, but they weren't *bad*. But after what happened with Larry, I felt completely worthless. After that, I got deeper and deeper into drug use and really had very little control over what I did. I actually tried to kill myself a couple of times."

"Jo, I think it's interesting that all this happened to you after an experience that basically devalued you as a woman. You gave *yourself* to someone, and he treated that as something of very little worth or value. And that's what you came to believe about yourself. And your behavior followed very naturally from there."

"That's pretty much right," agreed Jo.

"It seems to me we need to work at getting you back your sense of worth," I suggested.

"How do we do that?" queried Jo, interestedly.

"Well, honestly, I think the best place to go for that is God. I mean, who else knows your true value as a woman better than the one who made you. He created you, and he *loves* you. And while other men mistakenly thought *and convinced you* that you weren't worth much, God knows your true worth."

Jo nodded thoughtfully.

"Jo, I believe God's valuation of a woman is seen *most* clearly in the life of Jesus. Would you like to see a conversation that Jesus had with a woman in the Bible?"

"Sure."

"It comes from John chapter 8," I said, reaching for the Bible on my shelf.

"Oh, that must be the story of the woman caught in adultery," responded Jo.

"I see you're familiar with the Bible," I stated. We read through the story, and I pointed out how Jesus protected the vulnerable woman from the men who simply wanted to use her for their own ends. Then we noted how Jesus let the woman know that even though she had done wrong, she was not condemned by him.

"Jo," I asked, "would you like to take a moment to pray and ask God to restore your true worth to you? To heal you of the wound in your soul? That's what it is, isn't it? A wound on the inside?"

"Oh, big time!" replied Jo. Then, "Yes, I would like to pray about that. Do you want me to pray, or will you pray?" asked Jo, just a little nervously.

"It's not *my* wound," I replied with a smile.

"Right," replied Jo, returning my smile. "Should I pray out loud?"

"Sure. I like to join hands with people when I pray. Is that OK?"

"Yeah," said Jo, grasping my hands. She took a deep breath and then began. "Jesus, I am asking you to heal the wound in my soul. I really want to get back a sense of my own worth. Please forgive me for what I did. I know it was wrong. And I want to say that I forgive Larry too. Amen."

"Jo," I said, my head still bowed, "I have found that one very helpful way to heal from the past is simply to picture Jesus with us in the difficult moments of our past. Would you like to ask Jesus to help you see him there for you?"

"Yes, I would . . . Jesus, help me picture you there with me when I was hurting so much. I really want you to be with me and help me."

"Jo, is there one scene that comes to your mind that sort of encapsulates or sums up all the pain and devastation you felt from that experience when you were seventeen?"

"Yes, there is."

"Would you like to describe it to me?"

Jo went on, her head still bowed. "After we'd had sex the first time, we went back to a party, and Larry immediately got into a van with a bunch of other girls. Just before he left, we looked at each other right in the eyes, and he gave me this strange sort of smile."

"How did you feel?"

"I felt just *dead* inside."

"Mmm," I said, expressing my own hurt. "Jo, can you picture Jesus there with you?"

"Yes."

"Where is he in that scene?"

"I'm not sure, but he must have been there."

It seemed Jo was having trouble actually seeing Jesus's presence in her memory, so I went on with a few more questions. "Where did you go after Larry left?"

"I drank a whole pint of vodka, and then I *drove* home as fast as I could. And on a winding road! I think I was basically hoping I would die."

"Where did you end up?"

"I just remember getting home and Dad letting me in the door. That's all."

"Jo, as you think back over that whole sequence of events, is there a place you can actually see Jesus in the picture?"

Jo was silent for a moment. "Actually, I see him right beside me, with his arm around my shoulder."

"How does it feel to have Jesus there?"

"Good! And I can see him now in the car with me too, on the way home. He's sitting in the passenger seat. To tell you the truth, I see him in every scene now!"

"Cool! Is that a better way to leave that memory?"

"Way better!" Jo and I raised our heads and opened our eyes. "You know," Jo exclaimed, "I've prayed about this thing before, but I never saw it like that. It just feels totally different!"

"How does it feel?"

"Like the pain is gone inside!"

"Hey, that's just what you asked for, isn't it? Healing."

"Yeah. And I feel *stronger*. Like I'm not going to let that kind of thing go on any longer!"

"All right! And you don't have to!"

"You know, for so long, I've thought of myself as a victim. And it's like I'm *not* anymore!"

"Oh, Jo, I am so glad! Thank you, Jesus."

"Yes. Thank you, Jesus," concurred Jo.

Power for Parenting

Parenting is such a big job and an awesome task. God has entrusted his children into our hands for a period of years to care for them, teach them, and help shape their view of the world. And as we love them, discipline them, and encourage them, there will also come a time when we need to help them through difficult or scary experiences. Learning to take our fears to God is an important part of growing up as a disciple of Jesus. In the next two stories, I relate a couple of experiences I had helping our children learn to overcome their fears by the power of Jesus's presence.

ℰℂ

Chris: Danger on the River

One summer, my family and I vacationed in North Dakota and camped on the shores of the muddy Missouri River. During the day, my two small boys and I hiked out on the riverbed. The water level was quite low, and we could walk out on the mud-caked riverbed for almost a hundred yards before we reached the water's edge. As we approached the flowing water, the ground under our feet got more moist and spongy. Suddenly, my son Matthew sunk into the mud up to his knees. He turned and called to me for help! I reached out and grabbed his hand and helped pull him back onto more solid ground. I was surprised by how fast and how far Matthew had sunk into the mud, so I decided to test the ground with a tall walking stick I was carrying. I pushed the stick into the mud. It went down the entire length of the seven-foot stick and still did not hit a solid bottom!

Suddenly, I was petrified! "Back, boys!" I called, with obvious fear in my voice. I shuddered to think of what it would be like if the boys and I started to sink into soft mud that was clearly deeper than I was tall. So we hightailed it back to firm ground.

Days later, after returning home from our vacation, my son Chris called me into his bedroom one evening. He had been lying in bed for some time after we prayed and said good night, but he was having trouble falling asleep.

When I got into the room, I could see he was anxious and upset. "I'm having bad thoughts," he said, fighting back the tears.

"Do you want to tell me about it?" I asked.

"I can't stop thinking of when we were out by that river and Matthew started to sink into the mud. I *try* not to think about it, but I just can't help it!" Chris said as he began to cry.

I realized quickly that the fear I had expressed in my voice that day had terrified my son as well. "How about if we pray and ask Jesus to take those bad feelings away?" I suggested. Chris nodded and bowed his head. "Would you like to pray?" I said.

Chris began, "Dear Jesus, please take away these bad feelings I have about the time we were out by the river."

"Yes, Lord," I added, "please take away Chris's fears and help him with this memory. Amen."

"Chris," I added, "can you picture in your mind Jesus there with us by the river?"

"Uh-huh," said Chris, nodding.

"How do you see him?"

"He's got a white robe with a red thing over his shoulder, and he's got his hands on us, helping us get back to shore."

"How does it feel seeing him there?" I asked.

"Good," said Chris. "I feel OK now. I think I'll be able to go to sleep."

And he did. But not before I gave him a kiss and gave Jesus my thanks.

ഛ ഇ

Katie: Scary Movies

I believe that anything we see that is not according to the will of God can cause an emotional wound. Seeing anything that God does not want to happen can stir up in us emotions of anger, hate, or fear and can wound us emotionally. And the younger and more tender we are, the more seemingly trivial the thing that can cause an emotional wound.

Our daughter Katie, a fifth-grader, was a happy, cheerful child and had never had trouble going to sleep. So it concerned and surprised me one night when she came downstairs with tears in her eyes at 9:30 p.m. and reported that she couldn't fall asleep. She was having bad thoughts.

"What are you thinking about?" I asked.

"A movie I saw at my friend's house today."

Having begun to learn that the first stage of healing is to bring to light that which is hurting, I asked Katie, "Would like to tell me about the movie?"

Katie described a scene in which a phantom was playing an opera organ.

"Can you tell me what you see in that scene?" I asked Katie.

She replied, "There's a big organ, and it's playing by itself—scary music. And there's blood on the keys. I guess there's a man down underneath the organ in a trapdoor who's making it play. And then there's another time later on when he was walking up an old hallway, and there was a picture on the wall. There was a knife stabbed in the neck of the picture and blood flowing down."

Katie sat close to me as she told the scary scenes in her mind. I realized she had an emotional wound.

"Katie," I asked, "would you like to ask Jesus to help you with these fears and take them away?"

Katie nodded, a tear still in the corner of her eye.

"How about if we do this," I said. "How about if we pray and ask Jesus to come in and share that scary memory and be there so that he makes it not scary?"

"OK," said Katie.

Katie prayed and asked Jesus to help her not to be afraid.

"How about if we picture Jesus in that scene?" I asked. Where might we picture him?"

Katie looked intrigued by the idea but wasn't able to come up with an idea of how we could paint Jesus into the picture.

"Katie," I said, "you told me that there was a man underneath the organ. How about if we have Jesus lift up a trapdoor and reach down and take the hand of that man and bring him up? Should we do that?"

Katie nodded and said, "Yes."

"Can you picture that in your mind?" I asked.

She smiled and said, "Yes."

And then I remembered the blood on the keys of the organ. "Should we have Jesus take that blood off of there?"

Katie smiled again and nodded enthusiastically. So we pictured Jesus taking a cloth and wiping the blood off the keys so they were nice and clean.

Then I got another idea and suggested, "Katie, how about if we have Jesus sit down at the organ and play a nice song?"

Now she was beaming with joy.

I remembered that there was another scary scene that had troubled Katie, so I asked her if we should bring Jesus into the memory of the picture with a knife stabbed into it.

"Yes," said Katie.

"Let's see," I asked. "Can you picture Jesus walking up to that painting and gently drawing the knife out of it and then covering the picture with his hand? And when he moves his hand away, the blood is all gone and the picture is whole and the lady is smiling again."

"Yeah," said Katie.

It was clear by now that picturing Jesus in the scary scenes that were troubling her had brought Katie to a place of peace.

"Should we go up and tuck you into bed?" I asked Katie.

"Yes," she said.

And so, we walked upstairs, and as I sat on her bedside, we thanked Jesus that he is always with us. Then I clicked out the light, and Katie laid her head on her pillow. A big smile still lingered on her face, and she fell asleep effortlessly.

Kelly: Abortion

I met Kelly during her time of recovery at the treatment center. She began telling me of her early life: how she had an alcoholic dad and a very strong mom. She herself was very athletic in high school. But after high school she ended up in relationships with men who abused her. After she moved to Colorado, she got pregnant and got an abortion.

"Have you ever had a chance to talk with anyone about your abortion?" I asked.

"No," replied Kelly. "I don't think I can forgive myself."

"I don't think so either," I stated, leaning in a little and looking Kelly in the eye. "This thing is so big that only *God* could do that! I truly believe it would take a miracle to set you free from that guilt." I paused briefly. "Kelly, could I tell you what I believe about forgiveness?"

"Yes. Please," Kelly urged.

"First, I believe forgiveness involves facing the pain that our wrong actions have caused—the pain you've carried all these years. The pain of a baby who never got a chance at life. And for help to face that, I look to Jesus on the cross. There I see a God who suffers! A God who understands pain! I believe Jesus felt the pain of your actions and mine when he was there on the cross. He felt the physical pain of having his body torn to shreds. But even worse, he felt the emotional pain of all the wrongs people have ever done to each other. That's a lot of pain!" I said.

"Yeah, really," agreed Kelly.

"But secondly—and this is the amazing part about forgiveness—he is willing to not cut us loose or send us away for all the pain we've caused him and each other. He still accepts us and wants to release us from our guilt. Remember what Jesus said while he was hanging on the cross? 'Father, forgive them, they don't know what they are doing.' Kelly, when you got your abortion, did you know what you were getting yourself in for?"

"No!" Kelly began to cry, and I reached out and touched her arm while she wiped away her tears.

"Would you like to ask God to forgive you for what you did?" I offered.

Kelly took my hands and said, "God, please forgive me for what I did!" More tears were the conclusion of her prayer.

"Kelly," I said, "those memories can be hard things. Every time we think of them, they hurt us."

"Yes!" exclaimed Kelly.

"Would you like to pray again and ask Jesus to heal you—to be with you in that memory of your abortion?"

Kelly hesitated. "I usually pray alone in the woods. It's not easy to pray with someone else!"

I paused for a minute, not sure how to proceed. "Kelly, may I ask, what do *you* believe about Jesus?"

"That he's God's Son who died on the cross for me, just like you said."

There was another pause, and then I asked, "Another woman once told me that she was afraid if she ever faced her real emotions, she might not be able to *stop* crying. Do you ever feel like that?"

"Yes!" Kelly wrapped her arms around herself and looked down at the table. "This is like the hardest thing I've ever had to bear!"

"I agree with you, Kelly. I have never seen pain like that of a woman who's been through an abortion." I paused. "But I would *like* to see you healed."

There was a silence as both of us sat motionless and wordless for some time.

"Kelly, I feel like you're on the street in front of the abortion clinic, pacing back and forth, wanting to go in there and face what happened, but afraid to go through the doors. Is that how you feel?"

"Yes." Kelly paused for a moment longer and then began, "Well, I can see it *all*. I remember being on a table." The tears had returned as Kelly began her story. "Someone was pushing on my tummy. I remember seeing an ultrasound . . . seeing a baby's hands and feet. Then it was gone!"

Kelly dissolved in tears, and I reached out my arm and put it around her shoulder. Through the sobs, Kelly prayed, "Oh, God, please help me! I can't bear this alone! Please take away the hurt and let me heal."

After a moment or two, Kelly calmed down a bit, and I said, "Kelly, do you see Jesus anywhere in that picture?"

"Yes, he's holding my baby," replied Kelly with a new calmness. "There's light coming down from somewhere above."

"Can you picture him walking over beside your bed and reaching out to wipe the sweat from your forehead and stroke your hair?"

Kelly continued my sentence, "And that it's going to be all right and that he'll take care of my baby."

I was silent for a time, knowing we were at a very tender spot and wanting to go slowly. "Is that what he's telling you?" I asked.

There was no answer as Kelly seemed absorbed in herself. Then after a few minutes, she exclaimed, "I don't feel the pain anymore!" She opened her eyes, and I looked into them questioningly.

"What *do* you feel?" I asked.

"I feel . . . relief." Kelly looked aside as if she was searching through her emotions within.

"Is that a good place for this memory to end?" I asked.

"It's so wonderful," she replied, looking back at me with utter amazement in her eyes. "He just *took the pain away!*"

"That's exactly what you asked him to do, isn't it?" I said.

"Yes, it is!" Kelly replied.

"Only *he* can do that!" I marveled, smiling. "Thank you, Lord."

I love the Lord, for he heard my voice
He heard my cry for mercy
Because he turned his ear to me
I will call on him as long as I live
The cords of death entangled me
The anguish of the grave came upon me
I was overcome by trouble and sorrow
Then I called on the name of the Lord
"Oh Lord, save me"
The Lord is gracious and righteous
Our God is full of compassion
The Lord protects the simple-hearted
When I was in great need, he saved me
Be at rest once more, O my soul
For the Lord has been good to you
For you, Lord, have delivered my soul from death
My eyes from tears
My feet from stumbling
That I may walk before the Lord
In the land of the living

(Psalm 116:1-9)

෨ ෬

Jordan: Violent Death of a Loved One

Jordan was a tall black man who must have tipped the scales at over 250 pounds. He was in the process of recovery from alcoholism and talked with me in my office at the treatment center.

"I grew up with adoptive parents whom I loved very much," Jordan began. "My real dad was an alcoholic and a violent man from what I've been told. I never met him. And my biological mother died from complications two days after I was born.

"I felt lonely at first when I went to school because I was different from everybody else. But as I grew older and got into sports, I had lots of friends and everybody liked me."

We talked on, and Jordan got on the topic of losses in his life. He mentioned the loss of his grandfather.

"How old were you when your grandpa passed away?" I asked.

"About twenty-two," Jordan replied.

"Do you want to tell me how he died?"

"He was hit by a truck," Jordan explained. "He had stepped out into a street, and this truck was speeding by. The driver apparently didn't see him—I guess the sun was in his eyes. Anyway, he hit him straight on. I was called to identify my grandfather's body at the morgue. I thought I would be the strongest one, so I agreed to do it."

Then Jordan's eyes began to well up with tears and his body began to tremble. After a moment, he burst out, "His face was gone! He didn't even look like my grandpa!" Jordan hung his head and began to sob. I slid my chair closer and put my arm on his arm while Jordan cried for a few moments. I thought of how those tears were a very normal and natural expression of grief—some grieving that Jordan was not all the way through yet. Then I remembered something I had read recently about how Jesus even wants to help us carry our grief. As Isaiah said,

"He bore our griefs and carried our sorrows." After he quieted himself, I offered a thought.

"Jordan, the only thing that keeps me sane at moments like this is my belief that God understands what we're going through because he shared our sufferings. That's what I believe happened in the life of Jesus: God became a man and suffered all the pain that we've felt—all the sin of the world. Jesus suffered it when he died on the cross. He did it so he could be with you in your suffering!

"Jordan," I said, "I sometimes find peace by simply picturing Jesus with me at a difficult time in my life. Would you like me to pray for you and ask God to help you picture Jesus there with you?"

"I would like that!" responded Jordan. "Would you, please?"

"Jesus," I prayed, "I believe you shared all our suffering on the cross. And I believe you understand how much Jordan was hurt when his grandpa died. Would you please help Jordan to see you there when he saw his grandpa after the accident? We really need your help."

I paused briefly, and then with my eyes still closed and my hands still gripping Jordan's tightly, I asked Jordan, "Can you picture Jesus there with you?"

"Yes, I can," he replied.

"How do you see it?"

"He's standing right across from me, next to my grandfather's head."

"How does it feel with him there?"

"Better," answered Jordan. "Like he's there to take care of my grandfather now." He was crying slightly, but the tears were different from the wracking sobs he had cried earlier. They seemed to be tears of relief.

When we opened our eyes again, Jordan went right on with the conversation, switching to a new topic. I was surprised by this quickness and wondered if Jordan was still "running" from something connected with that memory. But I let him talk on for a while until later when the conversation returned to his grandfather. I took the opportunity to see how Jordan felt now.

"Do you feel that it was helpful to pray about your grandpa's death?" I asked.

"Oh man, yeah!" responded Jordan, with an intensity that surprised me.

"Can you still picture Jesus there?"

"Yes, he's right there next to my grandfather. And there's a kind of white glow all around him. And my grandfather looks different in my mind now. You see, when I saw him in the morgue, the whole left side of his face was just gone. But now, with Jesus there, his face is normal. I see him lying there like he was asleep."

I observed that Jordan was talking calmly now about the very memory that had made him sob with pain and grief only a few minutes ago. "So it feels different now?"

"Completely!" Jordan exclaimed. "I don't know what you did, but thank you!"

"I didn't do nothin'!" I objected. "I just suggested we take it to Jesus." I was about to ask Jordan if he would like to thank Jesus for what happened, but Jordan beat me to it. He spontaneously prayed, "Thank you, Lord, for helpin' me with this. And thank you that I can leave my grandfather with you!"

"Amen!" I said in agreement.

ఎఠ

Kate: Healing from Abortion

Kate was a twenty-four-year-old woman who'd had an abortion several months before we spoke. Tears filled her eyes as she told me how she'd suffered since the abortion.

"I feel like I have a hole in my heart."

She told me about her nightmares, her futile efforts to forget, and the tears that welled up every time she saw or heard about a newborn.

"I wonder if I will ever be able to forgive myself," Kate admitted.

"Kate," I said, "I think we're going to need God's help with this. May I ask what you believe about God?"

"I wasn't raised in a family that went to church. I guess I feel kind of cheated about that."

We talked about God and what he does to forgive us. "It all relates back to what happened with Jesus on the cross," I said. "Kate, if you came before a judge in court with something on your record, he would determine some fine or punishment for you to clear your record. Well, I believe that at the cross, God took all the wrongs that were on your record and mine and everyone else's and transferred them onto Jesus's record. Jesus willingly suffered and died serving *our* sentence. So now, God can look at us and say, 'I don't need to punish you for your wrongs. Someone has already served your sentence. I just want to love you and forgive you.'"

"That's beautiful!" Kate exclaimed.

"Would you like to ask God to forgive you for ending your baby's life?" I asked.

"Yes," Kate nodded. Through the sobs, Kate prayed from her heart, "Lord, I'm sorry for my sins. I'm sorry that I let go of the baby you gave me . . . Please forgive me!"

After a moment, I asked, "Kate, would you like to ask Jesus to help you heal from the memory of your abortion by picturing him there with you?"

Kate jumped back into prayer, "Jesus, please come and heal the memory of what happened to me when I went to the clinic."

Though I'd never been in an abortion clinic, I had heard other women describe their experience with abortions. In my mind, I saw Kate in a white hospital gown, lying on an operating table, trembling and terrified at what was taking place.

"Kate," I asked, "can you picture yourself lying on an operating table and Jesus standing next to you? He's holding your hand, and tears are streaming down his face because he knows how much this is hurting you. Can you picture that?"

"Yes, I can!"

I thought about the need to commit into God's hands the life of the child who had died.

"Then can you imagine Jesus there holding a little baby next to his shoulder?"

"Yes."

"Would you like to give that little baby a name?"

Kate told me she had an intuitive feeling her baby was a girl. "I'd like to name her April."

"Would you like to pray for April?" I asked.

"Jesus," Kate prayed, "thank you that you were there for April. Please take care of her and help me heal from letting her go."

After a break, I asked Kate, "How are you feeling now?"

"Content," she replied. "I actually feel light as a feather inside. I feel the presence of God a hundred times more powerfully than I ever have before!"

"Go with it, Kate. Follow his path. He will never lead you wrong!"

෨ CR

Todd: Homosexual Rape

I met Todd at the treatment center, and as we began our conversation, he described his life growing up.

"I came from a good Catholic family," began Todd. "My parents were both teachers. I myself wanted to join the Coast Guard. See, we had always lived inland, but I was fascinated by the sea and boats. So that's what I did. But then when I was in Arizona, I had kind of a homosexual experience." Todd paused for a moment.

"Want to tell me about it?" I asked.

"Well, I was temporarily separated from my wife at the time. I had gone to the southwestern states, and I was kind of bummed I couldn't see my son. So I went on a little traveling party tour. I met this guy in a bar one night, and he seemed real friendly, so I went home with him. I had been drinking pretty heavy and began passing out. Then I came to enough to realize he was performing oral sex on me. I felt revolted and left! I was sick after that for two days. My parents could see that something happened in Arizona because I wasn't the same after that. I felt ashamed, disgusted, and afraid I might get into that kind of thing again. I still have the memory of it that just haunts me!" Todd began to cry.

After a few moments, I began, "Todd, I believe there's three steps to healing from a story like this. To tell the story, to identify the feelings, and to pray and forgive. You've told me the story. And you've done a good job identifying your feelings. Would you like to pray and tell God you forgive that man for what he did?"

"Yeah, I would."

Todd prayed a simple prayer, telling God he forgave the man. Then I asked, "Would you like to pray and ask Jesus to help you picture him there in that scene? He promised in Matthew 28 in the Bible that he would always be with us."

Todd prayed, "Jesus, could you help me to see you there? I really want your help with this thing."

"Are you able to see him in that scene anywhere?" I asked.

"Yes, in the kitchen of that man's apartment. He's standing there, glowing!"

"How does it feel seeing him there?"

"It feels good! You know, I was crying out for God to get me out of there, and he *really* was *there* helping me out of that situation!"

"Can you picture him going out the door with you?"

"Yes."

"Is he communicating anything to you?"

"That it was not my fault. He knows I didn't want this to happen!"

There was a pause, and then I let Todd know what I was seeing in my mind. "Can you picture Jesus with his arm around you?"

"Yes. I see him walking with me now on the shore of the ocean."

"Ah," I sighed, "he knows how much you love the ocean."

We opened our eyes as our prayer time ended. I looked into Todd's face and saw a look of serenity. "Isn't it wonderful that Jesus can turn that nightmare into a beautiful, rich memory of time together on the shore with a Friend?"

"Yeah!" nodded Todd.

What You Don't See

There are a few things that you won't see on these pages that I would like to draw your attention to.

Firstly, I can't really portray the amount of time this kind of healing prayer actually takes. Each of these stories takes just a few minutes to read. But most are distilled from one to three hours of conversation. Sometimes the traumatic memory is more or less right on the surface and can easily be gotten to. But other times, it takes a long time of listening to get down to the place where people are stuck inside.

Secondly, you won't see in these pages the uncertainty that I feel when I am listening to someone talk and inwardly wondering, "Is this a subject I should dig into more deeply, or is this not that important?" Of course, certain subjects are pretty sure bets. When I hear a woman mention abortion, my ears perk up. But even there, I have talked to some postabortive women who didn't seem to be deeply troubled by it. Keeping my eyes and ears open to answer the question "Where is the person wounded?" takes a fair amount of work and wondering. I can only try to be sensitive to the Holy Spirit's guidance and attentive to people's body language and responses to my inquiries.

Thirdly, on paper, these conversations seem to shift into a discussion about Jesus and spiritual matters so smoothly. But in real life, that transition is almost always a difficult step for me. Most of these conversations were not in a church setting, so introducing Jesus into the conversation is a bit of a risk and a little scary (though less so over time). And yet I press through that fear because I am convinced that *only* Jesus is able to heal every wound no matter how deep it is or how long it has been carried.

I tell you these things so that as you step out in faith and offer the Good News of Jesus and his healing power to hurting people you know, you won't get discouraged. If it takes longer, seems more confusing, and strikes you as harder than it looked on paper, don't lose heart! Just do it with all the love that God gives you. And remember, your labor is never in vain in the Lord.

My sincere hope is that both you and I will learn from every opportunity we have to listen to people's hurts, to share the Good News of Jesus, and to pray with them for healing. And that we will do it better tomorrow than we do today.

৶ ଓ

Karen: Child Abuse

I had been having personal Bible study with Karen for a number of months. It was clear that the conviction was growing in her that Jesus was truly God's Son come to earth, to bring the Heavenly Father's love in a personal way. I knew that Karen had come from a troubled background, so I was glad one time at our Bible study meeting when she began talking about her past in a specific way. I thought we might help her move toward emotional healing.

"My mother was very harsh with us," Karen said. "She used to hit us a lot. I guess you would say she verbally abused us too. I remember the time when I was fourteen . . . when I left home. My mom had lost control and beat me up pretty bad. She had to take me to the doctor and have him tend to the cuts and bruises on my face. When I was alone with him, the doctor asked me how this had happened. I wasn't sure what to say. I thought if I told the truth, the doctor would take me away from my mom, and I didn't want that. So I made up some story about having fallen down the steps. But I don't think he believed me. I remember how he looked at me and said, 'I'm going to make sure that you get the help that you need.' From there, I talked to a social worker, and later that day, they came and picked me up at my house and took me away. I was taken to a girls' school. I remember sitting all alone in a big room. What hurt me most was the nagging question in my mind: Does *anybody* love me?"

I could see that the rejection and pain caused by the beatings Karen had taken and by the separation from all that she knew still left a deep emotional wound inside.

"Karen," I said, "I'm coming to believe that Jesus wants to share with us our most painful moments and memories. He wants to help heal the hurt by being there *with us*. Would you like to pray with me and invite Jesus to be with you in that memory of sitting all alone, wondering if anyone loved you?"

"Yes, I would," said Karen.

So we joined hands and bowed our heads.

"Karen, can you picture yourself in that room as a fourteen-year-old girl all alone wondering about love . . . wondering if anyone loved you?"

Karen nodded.

"Can you picture Jesus there with you?" I asked.

There was a long pause, and Karen said, "Not really."

Then I remembered, we hadn't yet prayed. So I said, "Karen, how about if we pray? Would you like to *ask* Jesus to be there with you, to let you see him there?"

"Jesus," Karen prayed, "please let me see you there with me when I was hurting as a girl."

"Can you picture him there now?" I asked hopefully.

"Yes, I can," said Karen.

"Where is he in your memory?" I asked.

"He's standing right above me."

"What does he look like?"

"He's got a long white gown, and his hair is just shining."

"How does it feel to have him there?" I asked.

"Better," she replied. "It's kind of comforting."

"Karen," I said, "can you picture Jesus reaching out and putting his hand on you?"

"Yes, I can," said Karen.

Now there were tears in her eyes and a quivering in her voice. I paused for a moment, and then I described what I was seeing in my own imagination.

"Karen, can you picture Jesus taking you up in his arms and holding you?"

"I'm already there," she replied. "He is holding me."

"Can you feel the warmth of his love flowing from his hands into your body?" I asked.

"Yes, I can," she said.

Then I thought of one last thing. "Karen, you said your face was bruised and cut. Can you picture Jesus touching you with his hands on your face and healing those cuts?"

"Yes," she said. "I can feel warmth."

"Is that a good place for that memory to end?" I asked.

"Yes," Karen said with a big sigh of contentment.

After a quiet moment, we both opened our eyes and smiled at each other.

"That was awesome," said Karen. "I could actually *feel* Jesus's hand healing my face. I could feel the warmth! I've only experienced anything like that one other time. I was driving in the car once after I hurt my back, and I prayed for God to heal my back. I literally felt a warmth spread throughout my back. After that, the pain was gone. But as we pictured it, I could feel that same healing warmth from the touch of Jesus."

The effects of Karen's emotional healing seemed to extend into other areas of her life. Her faith seemed to take a huge leap forward. A few days after this experience, Karen was relating to me how she was talking with her sister on the phone.

"I told my sister that I really believe in Jesus, and I'm taking the road of being his follower now. I told her that doesn't conflict in any way with my being Indian because Jesus came with love for all people."

I was so thrilled that Karen was now identifying herself as a believer in Jesus.

Another mysterious happening occurred about two weeks later when Karen related to me, with utter amazement in her voice, that she had gotten a letter on her birthday. It was a birthday card from her mother. Inside was a letter stating something she had *never* heard from her mother—apologies for the many times she had mistreated her through the years. Karen said she could hardly believe what she was reading! And she had a good phone conversation with her mother subsequent to reading the letter.

I was simply left to wonder how in God's amazing providence the step of inner healing for Karen might have fit together with the work of God in Karen's mother as he brought her to a place of seeking forgiveness from her daughter whom she had wounded so badly. Now healing was coming not only to Karen's emotions but also to her relationship with her mother as well.

ℰℭℛ

Jack: Violence against Women

Jack was a 40 year-old man I had met in jail. He had been incarcerated for about seven months and, during that time, had become a Christian. We were visiting through the glass in the visitation booth one night when Jack told me he was having a hard time maintaining a personal connection with God.

"I been struggling lately, Mark. I tried writing down my prayers like you suggested last week, but they just don't seem right. I've worked my way past the obstacle of Jesus being God—I see that now. But I'm stuck as far as having a personal relationship with God. I feel good when I come talk with you or the other brothers, but when I'm by myself, I just sink back down."

I wanted to see how Jack understood his own identity before God, so I asked him, "Jack, if Jesus would come to you and look you right in the eyes, what do you think he would say to you? How would he feel about you?"

"How would he feel about *me*? Wow! I would wish he would love me and all. But honestly, with all that I've done, I don't see how he couldn't hate me."

We paused for a minute, and I thought Jack's heart was softening as he went on, "Sometimes I think that I've done too much—that I'm too far gone." (Jack had admitted to me before that his past had involved a lot of selling drugs and violent living.)

"I'm glad to hear you say that, Jack. I mean, it's good to get that thought out in the open. Now who do you suppose is feeding you that thought? Who wants you to think 'You're too far gone! There's no hope for you!'"

"The devil."

"I think so too. And the devil is more than happy to use our past against us. Jack, how would you feel if I prayed and asked the Holy Spirit to bring to your mind *one thing* from the past that you did wrong—something the devil can point to in order to make you think you're beyond hope? Then we can give that experience to God and ask him to forgive you for it so the devil can't use it against you anymore."

"Sure, go ahead."

I prayed for God to reveal one thing to Jack that could be brought into the light and forgiven. "Anything come to mind?" I asked.

"Well, the only thing in my mind right now is all the bad stuff I've done to women . . . all the girlfriends I've had . . . and my mother—how I've taken advantage of her and all that she's done for me."

I wanted to help Jack get specific about his wrongs, so I asked, "Jack, is there any specific experience that comes to your mind when you think of this?"

"Yes, there is. It was with my last girlfriend. We were in bed one night and she said something and I punched her, right in the head. I mean, I hit her like you hit a man! Just wham! And she kind of curled up in the fetal position. I thought maybe I'd killed her. God, I felt awful! I mean, I've fought a lot of men before, but you just don't hit a woman!" Jack's eyes were misty.

"Would you like to pray and ask God to forgive you for what you did that night?"

"I don't think I could forgive *myself*!" Jack replied.

I knew we had to head straight to the cross of Jesus now. "Jack, Peter wrote in the Bible that Jesus bore our sins—he carried our sins, he felt them—on the cross so that we could die to sin and live the right way—in *right*eousnes. Now if I understand that right, it means that part of what Jesus suffered on the cross was the pain you gave your girlfriend that night. He felt that punch right with her so that he could honestly say to you, 'I know what you've done, and I forgive you. You don't have to carry that one anymore!' Does that make sense, Jack?"

"I just don't know if I can let it go."

"And that's why he suffered our sins—so that we could let it go . . . so that we could 'die to sin and live to righteousness.'"

"I guess I feel like *I* have to suffer for my own sins."

"I see. But the Bible says Jesus suffered *for you* just so that you wouldn't have to be stuck there, doing that."

"Hmm," replied Jack. He stared quietly into space for a moment or two. I sat looking at his eyes and *prayed* that God would open his eyes to see that what Jesus did was for *his* forgiveness.

"OK, I'd like to pray and ask the Father to forgive me."

"Go ahead," I said.

"Dear Father and Jesus, I need your help with what I did to my girlfriend. Please forgive me for hitting her, and help me to let go of it."

"Yes, Lord," I added. "Thank you that Jesus took our sins on that cross so that we don't have to carry them anymore. Thank you so much for your forgiveness."

"Jack, sometimes I find it a very healing experience to actually picture Jesus there with me in my worst moments—to see him there helping me through it. Would you like to ask Jesus to help you picture him there with you that night when you hit your girlfriend?"

"Yeah." Then Jack prayed, "Jesus, I want to see you there, 'cause I really need your help with this thing about my girlfriend."

"Can you picture yourself in that bed where you hit your girlfriend?"

"Oh yeah!"

"Can you see Jesus there with you?" I asked.

"Yes, I can."

"How does he look?"

"He's wearing a long robe, and he's kind of shining," replied Jack.

"How does it feel with Jesus there?"

"Good! It's not so dark anymore. It's like, with Jesus there, the whole thing isn't all darkness like it was before."

I thought of John's words in the opening of his Gospel: "The light shines in the darkness, and the darkness has not overcome it."

⋘ ⋙

Carol: Sexual Experimentation

Carol was a short heavy woman with a pretty face who was at the treatment center recovering from her alcoholism. She told me she had gone through an outpatient program for alcoholism a few years ago, but she hadn't "gotten it all out."

"There were a few things that I thought just God could handle," she admitted. "But I want to get it all out now."

Carol began her story, telling me how she had been molested by an uncle when she was a young child. Her father was an alcoholic, and she was not close to her mother.

"I guess you could say us kids kind of raised each other," said Carol. "I think I turned to sex to fill the void. I slept with boys thinking it would make them like me. Then I did some pretty weird things that I really felt bad about." Carol paused momentarily. "The way I look at it now, a pet was just like being part of the family . . . almost like another human being. I mean, they have feelings too." Carol paused again.

"And . . . you had some sexual experiences with a pet?" I asked gently.

"Yes," replied Carol, looking shamefully at the floor.

I assured her that she wasn't the only one I knew who had had such experiences. And in my mind, I knew there was a story here, *crying* to be told.

"Would you like to tell me what happened?" I asked Carol.

She went on to relate two instances that had occurred when she was just a girl and then concluded, "I felt so dirty and afraid."

Moving to a related subject, Carol went on, "I also have a terrible time with masturbation. I know it's wrong, and I tell God I'm sorry, but then I do it again. And it's gotten to the point where I don't even think he's listening anymore. Doesn't it say somewhere in the Bible that if we keep committing the same sin, he'll spit us out of his mouth or something?"

I told Carol that nowhere in the Bible is masturbation considered as a sin—the Bible says virtually nothing about it.

"But the Bible *does* address sexual experience with animals," I stated. "What does that tell us? I think it tells us that God knew that it's one of those things that would be a temptation—that would trip some of us up and leave us feeling stuck in a mess. And I believe it was to rescue us from those messes we humans get ourselves into that God came among us in the person of Jesus." I continued. "May I ask what *you* believe about Jesus?"

"I believe that he died on the cross for our sins. And that he will forgive us if we ask him and really intend to change," said Carol.

"That he loves you?" I questioned.

"Yes."

"Carol, would you like to pray and talk to God about this matter and picture him there to forgive you?"

Carol nodded and reached out to take my hands as we bowed our heads to pray. "God," she said, "you know how much this has bothered me all these years, how dirty I have felt inside. Please forgive me for what I did. Thank you for letting me talk this over with Pastor Mark and for him letting me know that I'm not the only person this has happened to."

Carol ended her prayer but remained silent. I asked her softly, "Carol, can you still picture the place where this happened?"

"Yes," Carol responded. "I'm in my bedroom, lying softly on my bed."

"If Jesus were to enter into that memory, where would he be?"

"I'm not sure what you mean."

"Can you picture Jesus standing in the doorway?" I asked.

"Yes."

"Can you imagine him coming and sitting on the edge of your bed?"

"Yes."

"How do you feel?"

"A little ashamed . . . nervous."

"Can you imagine him reaching out and cupping your cheeks in his hands, lifting your face up so he can look into your eyes, and saying, 'I don't condemn you. I know how bad this made you feel, and I forgive you and want to wash it away from your soul because I love you'?"

Then in my own mind, I saw Jesus hugging this little girl. "Carol, can you imagine Jesus wrapping his arms around you and drawing you to himself in a tight hug?" Carol had begun to cry softly as soon as I related Jesus's words, "I don't want to condemn you." But when she pictured Jesus hugging her, Carol let loose with a torrent of sobs and tears of relief. I knelt beside her chair and held her tightly while she cried. When the tears had subsided, I sat back in my chair.

"Thank you," she said, drying her eyes. "That felt *so* good. I could just *picture* Jesus hugging me! I've carried that for so long. It's such a relief to be rid of it!"

ഇരുഃ

Lisa: Multiple Wounds

Lisa was a twenty-nine-year-old woman, half-black and half-white (a racial combination that had made her feel excluded all her life), whose long black wavy hair encased a beautiful face with olive skin. She was doing a fifth step with me and admitted that she wanted to talk about some of the things that had happened in her past that still bothered her—still kept her abusing drugs and alcohol.

"My brother molested me when I was young, between the ages of three and six, and I think that still bugs me," she stated early in our conversation. "I think it affected me later too because when I got older, I kind of slept with any man who wanted to. I think I felt like I was already ruined, so what the heck."

Knowing that the first step to healing is always to be able to tell the story, I asked, "Would you like to tell me what happened with you and your brother—what memories stick in your mind?"

"Well it started when my older brother..." and Natalie began to tell me about her abuse. After briefly describing what her brother had done, she said, "I didn't like it and didn't think it was right, but he said that's how an older brother showed his love. The abuse went on for three years until one time my mother walked in on us. She threw him against the wall and told him never to do that again...and he never did. I was thankful to Mom for that."

"But partly, I think, because of what my brother did, we all got put in foster homes after that. The first place I got treated badly. But my mother complained to social services and got me placed in another home with a really neat lady named Jackie. She was a saint! She took me to church for the first time in my life. I liked her."

Lisa went on to describe how she'd gone back home at age twelve and had begun using drugs and alcohol.

"Then when I was about fourteen, my best friend got killed. We were out on a street corner, selling some dope, and a car came by with some gang members. I remember I yelled at her to get down. But before she could move, I felt the bullet go by me and hit her in the back of the head. She went down in a pool of blood. She died in my arms. That's when I stopped believing in God."

"I'm sorry," I said softly.

"After that, my drinking really increased. Up until I was about sixteen, and I got raped—twice! Then it increased even more!"

"Do you want to tell me what happened with the rapes?" I asked.

"Well, the first time, I was walking down an alley in South Minneapolis when some guy just grabbed me and pulled me into a yard. I fought him and screamed, but he stuffed something in my mouth so I couldn't make any noise. I fought more, and he punched me in the face. He had a knife and, when I kept fighting, he stabbed me in the side and threatened to kill me. After that, I just went limp and let him do his thing. When he left, I felt my side and my hand was full of blood. I got to a friend's house, and they took me to the hospital. But they never found the guy who did it."

Lisa was quiet, and I hesitated to go on but got up my courage and said, "How about the second one?"

"That time, I was selling drugs, and a guy invited me in someplace. I remember thinking 'Don't go with him.' But I did, and as soon as we were inside, he pulled out a gun and held it to my head. I did what he said."

"Lisa," I said, "you've had some *tough* experiences! First, the abuse by your brother. Then the death of your friend. Then getting raped. And then raped again." I paused, thinking how the next step was to identify feelings. "Would you like to go through each of those experiences again and tell me how they made you feel?"

"OK," replied Lisa.

"Let's start with the experience of being molested by your brother. How did that make you feel?"

"Dirty. I know there were times when I was a little girl when I pleaded with my mom to wash me because I just felt dirty. There were times when I would scrub my arms so hard they would actually bleed. I just couldn't seem to get clean."

Lisa paused for a moment and then continued, "And confused. I know I felt confused."

"Because he told you he was loving you when he was molesting you?"

"Yes. I was only three! And he was so much older. But I remember thinking the first time he did it when I was only three, and I didn't even know anything about sex—I remember thinking 'This is not right!' And I felt guilty."

I was stunned that she should feel guilty, yet I recalled how often victims of sexual abuse take responsibility for the wrong. I wanted to try to help her sort out this matter, so I asked, "What did you do wrong in this experience that made you feel guilty?"

"I didn't tell anybody. And I knew I should have. But my brother told me that if I ever said anything about this, our family would be split up—they would take us all away from our mother. And I didn't want to cause that! I know now this was wrong. People tell me it wasn't my fault. But . . ." Lisa's voice trailed off, not quite able to explain the vague feelings of guilt that lingered.

"You know," I replied, "the lies that your brother told you and the fear of breaking up your family that these lies caused, acted kind of like an invisible gag tied around your mouth to keep you from talking, didn't they?"

"Wow, I've never thought of it like that. But that's exactly how it felt—like I was gagged!"

"Any other feelings?" I asked.

"Fear."

"Of what?"

"Oh, I don't know . . . going to hell, I guess. I just felt I had this terrible thing in my life that was *wrong*."

Lisa paused, and after a while, I asked about her feelings relating to the murder.

"When my friend died, I felt like part of me died with her."

"Part of your heart?" I asked.

"Yeah. She was like a sister to me. We'd grown up together and played together ever since I was four years old. We were planning to go to nursing school together when we got older. In fact, she was the only one I ever told about my brother molesting me. I told her what was going on." Lisa laughed nostalgically as she went on, "We made plans to tie him up and beat him with a bat . . . but we couldn't do anything like that. He was too big."

"You two were really close! I can see why you felt part of you died too."

Lisa was quiet, so I moved on to the next experience, "How about the rapes?"

"The first one I felt afraid . . . and alone . . . like there was nobody to watch out for me."

My heart sank at her words.

"And the second?"

"Like whatever! I guess I just felt like it was hopeless."

"Like whatever remained of your heart was just put under a boot and ground into the dirt?"

"Yeah, that's about it."

"Lisa, it seems to me your heart has taken a real beating through the years . . . Maybe it's kind of broken right now. But I'd like to see your heart healed. I'd like to see you get your heart back . . . whole again. And honestly, I believe Jesus is the only one who can do that—heal a heart. See, I believe Jesus felt the pain of all our sins when he died on the cross, and he forgave us all. It literally killed him. It crushed his heart. But after he died, he came back to life again. And I believe he is the only one who can help us by understanding our pain, and by bringing back to life the things inside us that have died. May I ask what you believe about Jesus?" I queried.

"Well, I believe he is able to save us . . . that he can heal my heart if I give it to him. Actually, I was alone in my bedroom a few days ago, thinking about this. I realized that I do need him, and I asked him into my heart. I remember the thought coming into my head after that: 'Things will be OK.' I guess I felt . . . peace."

"Lisa, would you like to invite Jesus to come with you back into those memories of your painful experiences and be with you there . . . ask him to heal your heart and put the broken pieces back together again?"

"Yes, I would." We joined hands, and Lisa prayed, "Jesus, please heal my heart. Come into my bad memories. I need your help to get over what happened to me."

"Lisa," I said, my head still bowed, "is there one scene that sort of sums up what took place between you and your brother?"

"Yes. When my mom walked in on us."

"Can you see Jesus there with you?"

"Yes," Lisa answered, "he's above me."

"How does he look? How does he feel about what's going on?"

"He has tears in his eyes. I see sadness and pain on his face."

"Does he do anything or say anything?"

"No," replied Lisa quietly.

I wanted to help Lisa picture Jesus actively rescuing her, so I described what I saw in my mind. "Can you imagine him coming down to cover you? And as he does, he kind of displaces your brother?"

"Yes! I see him holding me! *Really* loving me!"

"And, Lisa, can you imagine Jesus leading you out of that room, out into the outdoors and taking you to a place where the sun is bright and the grass is green and there's a calm pool of water? Jesus invites you to swim in that pool. And as you go in and the water washes over your body, all the yuck and pain and shame of what your brother did to you is washed away from your heart! And when you come back to Jesus on the grass, he offers you a fresh white gown, and when you put it on, you look and feel *radiant*! Can you imagine that?"

"Yes!" Lisa said softly.

"How does that feel?"

"Good!"

"What about the memory with you and your girlfriend who was shot—can you see Jesus with you there?"

"Yes. He's standing beside me with his hand on my shoulder. He's telling me everything is going to be OK because he's there with me."

I thought of what Lisa had said about a part of her heart dying with her girlfriend. And I wondered if there was some way to communicate Jesus's desire to bring that part of her heart back to life again. I explained what I pictured in my mind. "Lisa, can you imagine Jesus taking you by the hand and walking you a little way away from that crime scene? Then you notice that in his *other* hand, Jesus has your girlfriend walking with him. But there, with Jesus, she is happy and beautiful. And Jesus swings the two of you together so you can embrace each other. And there, as Jesus holds the two of you together, you get some of your heart back. Does that make sense, Lisa?"

"Yes!" replied Lisa deeply.

I thought that Lisa was responding well and soaking up Jesus's healing love, so I decided to go right on to the next painful memory. "Lisa, how about the rape . . . What does Jesus do with that?"

Lisa's eyes were still closed, but she spoke strongly now, "He comes and picks that guy up off me! He's there for me. Somebody is *finally* there for me!"

"Can you see him touching your side where that guy stabbed you and healing you?"

"Yes," exclaimed Lisa, "I was already thinking that! And he hugs me!" Lisa's voice was becoming full and rich and strong.

"What about the second rape? Can you see Jesus there?"

"Yes. He takes the gun from that man and breaks it with his hand. That guy runs away in fear! But I know *I* don't have to be afraid now because he's going to be with me always."

"Lisa," I said, "I picture you in that scene now, and I see your heart is big, red, full, and pumping strong!"

"Yes!" exclaimed Lisa.

We both stood up and hugged each other.

Then we sat down again and Lisa said, "It's amazing . . . I feel *whole* again! Actually, I've never felt like this before. You know, I've had this dream a lot lately of me alone in a room with a bottle in my hand . . . and that's where I die—alone with a bottle. But I don't think it's going to go that way now!"

"Can you imagine Jesus stepping into that room with you, taking that bottle out of your hand and pouring it out onto the ground? 'You don't need this anymore,' he says. 'You have me! I will never leave you . . . now I will be *in* you.'"

"Yeah!" exclaimed Lisa with a smile.

ℴℴ

Mitch: Incest

Mitch was a forty-five-year-old man involved in a program of recovery from drug and alcohol abuse. His dark hair was cropped at the ear and was just beginning to gray. As he sat down in my office to do his fifth step, he explained the reason for his apparent nervousness.

"I haven't held anything back," he said, referring to the story of his life that he had written out to share with me. "I've put everything in here—thing's I've never told *anyone* about. I don't know how I'm ever going to face you again after I tell you these things. But, hey, I probably will never see you again, right? I just hope it will really help me to feel better like everyone says. Do you think it will?"

"It's helped millions of others. But you'll have to be the judge of that," I replied.

"Well, I'm *going* to tell it all!" he stated.

"Would you like to pray before we start?" I asked. Mitch said he would and prayed fervently to Jesus for help in being honest.

"Want to get started?" I invited.

Mitch told me about his early childhood with amazing realism. The weekends were "cartoon days." The school bus was "the big yellow car that took us to the brick building where a different mommy took care of us." The church was "the happy place where I got to go and play with different toys."

"I went back and looked through my eyes as a child when I wrote this," Mitch explained. He went on to tell about his sexual feelings awakening.

"I felt something new and funny inside when I would just look at the girls at school." His sexual feelings became stronger, and he began to masturbate regularly. He dreamed of having sex with the girls at school, but none of them wanted much to do with him (he was eleven years old). Then he hesitated.

"Oh boy. Do I really want to tell this part?" He paused and took a deep breath. "OK. I'm *going* to tell it. When I was eleven and my sister, Carol, was twelve, she wrote me a note one day, telling me to meet her at the pump house near the lake. When we got there, she began talking with me about school and how she felt about boys. We talked on, and she began talking about us and how we felt close to each other. By then, I could see what she was getting at, and I was terrified. But we talked on, and pretty soon. I gave in. We had sex with each other there in the pump house. Afterward I felt afraid, dirty, ashamed, appalled, disgusted, hopeless. I figured I had just lost whatever chance I had of going to heaven. And we continued to have sex till I was fifteen. My gosh, I can't look you in the face now!"

"Mitch," I asked, "would you like to take some time and pray about this—to ask Jesus to take away that heavy load of shame you feel?"

"Yes, I would! Can he do that?" Mitch asked.

"Oh, yes. He can do amazing things," I replied. "Would you like to pray and confess this to Jesus and ask him to be with you in that painful memory?"

"OK. Dear Jesus, please forgive me for what I did with my sister when we were young. And please come into this memory and help me, take away the shame I feel."

"Yes, Lord," I added. "I pray you would meet Mitch here and bring your light and your truth into this situation. Mitch, can you picture Jesus there in the pump house with you?"

"Yes, I can," he replied.

"How do you see him?"

"He's right there in the corner. This is amazing. I can see him right there."

"How does it feel with him there?"

"Different. Very different. It feels *clean.* It's like I can't even see myself there anymore, just him. I mean, I know I'm there, but all I can see is him . . . and my sister, Carol. But I only see her from the neck up. My gosh!" said Mitch suddenly looking at me. "I can't even remember what we did there. I mean, I know what we did there, but I can't for the life of me picture it in my memory anymore! I just see Jesus."

"Maybe that's a detail he wants to wash away for you."

"This is great! And I can look at you! I never thought I could do that, but I don't feel bad looking at you now. As a matter of fact, I feel closer to you now! This is amazing!" Mitch exclaimed.

"He's quite a Savior!" I replied.

Mitch went on to tell how his best friend, Cal, had led him into a homosexual relationship that lasted for a few weeks before Mitch put a stop to it. Also during this time, Mitch had gone to a summer Bible camp and had given his life to Christ.

"I was absolutely convinced I would never sin again. I read my Bible, worked hard, and didn't go out partying with the other kids from school. But then one day it happened.

"I went looking for Cal and heard he was out at a certain deserted farm place. When I got there, I could see his truck near the barn. My motorcycle wasn't running well and choked off, so I just coasted up quietly and parked my bike. I walked in on him and he was . . ." Mitch paused for a minute. "He was having sex with an animal! I yelled at him and asked him what was he doing that for! We talked for a while, and then . . . I did the *same thing he had done.* Afterward, I got on my bike and drove away.

I felt horrible, detestable, filthy, hopeless, condemned. I drove out into a field and *threw* my bike down. I cried and cried and begged God to forgive me. Oh man, I just feel awful thinking about it! I makes me sick!"

"Mitch, do you think we should pray about this too?"

"I don't know if I can! Yes, yes, let's pray!"

We joined hands and bowed our heads. Mitch prayed, "Oh, Lord, please come into this memory and heal me from this terrible thing that I did. I'm so sorry."

"Mitch," I asked, "can you see Jesus there with you?"

"He's standing a little ways away from me there in the field where I dumped my motorcycle. He has his arms stretched out to me. And all around him, the earth isn't dried up and dead like it was before in my memory. The ground is freshly plowed up and . . . like everything is *alive*."

"Do you see or think of anything else?" I asked.

"I see Cal kneeling and praying. He's not part of the scene with Jesus and me in the field. I just see him kneeling in prayer."

"How does that make you feel?"

"Good because, well, I really resented Cal after that. But now, I feel OK toward him. I realize he was probably sorry for what happened too. And the truth is, one week after that event, I took Cal to an evangelistic crusade, and we both went forward. He gave his life to Christ, and I rededicated myself to God. But we never did talk about what happened."

Mitch and I had lunch together later. During our meal, Mitch looked at the flowers on our table and the trees out the window, and he said to me, "This is really strange, but the colors look brighter to me now than they ever did before. I can't explain it very well, but everything looks more colorful to me now!"

Later we met back at my office to talk some more. Mitch said, "You know what I told you about the colors being brighter? I'm experiencing something else too. You know what tunnel vision is. Well, I feel like spiritually I've been looking through a tunnel all my life. And now I've come out and can see things all around me. It's like my peripheral vision has been restored."

I couldn't help but think that the secret sins that had made Mitch's world a dim and narrow place had been brought into the light of Jesus. And the truth had set him free.

But Does It Last?

Praying about our worst nightmares and suddenly seeing Jesus there with us can have a powerful and dramatic effect on us. But does it last?

One thing I'd like to highlight is the fact that when people see Jesus in their experiences, he invariably brings them a sense of peace. This way of praying does not produce some emotional high that somehow has to be sustained. Rather, it brings a calm, settled peace—the simple knowledge that all is now well because Jesus is here. And I know in my own experiences, once I see Jesus in a situation, he's there to stay. In fact, 100 percent of the time when I have checked back with people who have prayed and seen Jesus in their traumatic memories, I have been told they can still feel the peace of seeing him there. The memory never reverts back to the way it was before, and it never regains its power to induce fear, shame, guilt, or whatever negative emotion it initially held.

In the following two stories, you will hear from a couple of people who I checked back with to see how their healing prayer played out over the long haul.

☙ ❧

Dan: Teacher Abuse

Dan was a friend of mine who was a devoted believer in Jesus. He was a professional and had a wonderful family. He called me one day to ask if we could meet to talk about some personal problems. We agreed to meet at a local park to talk together. During our conversation, we surfaced a painful episode from Dan's past and prayed about it.

About a year later, I was visiting with Dan and asked him about our conversation.

"You remember that conversation we had in the park last summer, Dan? Would you say that has had any continuing benefit for you?"

"Oh, extremely!" replied Dan.

"Would you mind telling me what you remember from that conversation, and how it has helped you?" I requested.

"Sure," began Dan. "Well, I was having some conflict with one of my in-laws. They had poked fun at me for not being able to do something well and that really stirred up a lot of anger in me. I had called you to see if you could help me work through my anger issues. When we met and I explained the situation, you suggested that sometimes the emotions we feel can be influenced by events from the past. So you prayed with me that God would help me to see anything from my past that might be fueling my anger.

"After you prayed, I remember I closed my eyes, and all I could see was red. Then I kind of zeroed in on junior high, on my sixth-grade year. I had a teacher that year that spoke rudely to all the boys in the class. He used to go on and on about us not being smart enough to beat the girls on the tests. He always let the top student sit in a seat of honor at the front, and I *wanted* that seat. But far worse was the way he would constantly ridicule us for not being smart enough! I hated it!

"Then we went back to prayer, and you introduced Jesus into the situation. We were back in the classroom, and you asked me if I could see Jesus in that picture. I said, 'Yes, he's in the doorway.' I remember seeing myself in my desk, and then I saw Jesus walk up to my teacher (all the rest of the students were gone now). Jesus told my teacher that what he did in ridiculing us was wrong, and he needed to apologize to me for it. Then Jesus had me come forward, and my teacher apologized for hurting me. Then Jesus took me, and we walked out of the room. And I remember crying as I saw all this take place."

"So this released a lot of emotion that was trapped inside regarding this event?" I checked.

"Yes, it did."

"Can you remember exactly what point brought the tears out?"

"When my teacher apologized to me," answered Dan.

"And you say that prayer seems to have helped you since then?"

"It's been extremely healing. I've been much better in my anger issues. Not perfect! But *much* better."

"I can't tell you how glad I am to hear that, Dan."

"I can't tell you how glad I am to say it!" stated Dan with a smile.

ഔ ൬

Jamie: Death of a Sibling

Jamie was a friend of mine from a church my family used to attend. We were at her and her husband's house one evening for a party. I hadn't seen Jamie for some time. As the evening wore on and the crowd thinned, I found myself sitting with Jamie and her husband at their dining-room table. When I asked how she had been, Jamie admitted that she'd been having some health problems and things were kind of rough spiritually too. Instead of just nodding and changing the subject, I asked more questions about what Jamie was facing. Before long, we had hit upon a core belief.

"I know it sounds silly," Jamie said, "but I just have a hard time believing that God really loves me."

"Wow, that's something," I responded. "Can you say how long you've felt this way . . . when this began?"

Jamie went on to tell how she thought it went way back to her childhood and the death of her brother when she was five. We ended up praying to invite Jesus into the memory Jamie had of her brother's funeral. When we were done, it was midnight, and we headed home from the party.

It was a year before I saw Jamie again. (We had moved to a different city.) We were at her house for a party again. But this visit afforded no opportunity to talk in depth. Still, it made me remember our conversation from a year ago. So a few days later, I phoned Jamie to find out how things had gone after we had prayed about her painful memories.

Our phone call began with a few pleasantries, and then I came to the point of my call. "Jamie, I was just wondering how things had been going for you relating to the things we prayed about last year at your party."

"Good. Really good!" replied Jamie. "In fact, I would say it really changed my life!"

"Wow, that's great!" I exclaimed. "You know, I remember the general outline of what we prayed about . . . something with your brother's death when you were young. But could you just go over how you remember our prayer that night?"

"Sure! Well, you know you asked me how I was doing. And I remember wrestling inwardly, thinking, 'OK, Jamie, are you really gonna say what you feel?' I was afraid you'd think I was insane! But I knew I could trust you. And I could see you really wanted to know the truth. So I thought, 'OK, I'm gonna say this!' I was scared but excited that maybe somebody would understand what I'm going through. For years, I'd kind of touched on things relating to what was really going on in my heart. But it seemed most people just didn't get it. It was hard to admit too because I was a theology/psychology major, and I was having trouble believing God could really love me! Anyway, I felt very vulnerable but just started to talk honestly.

"I told you how since childhood, I never really trusted that God would be there for me . . . After all, he wasn't there for me then."

"By 'then,' you mean when your brother died," I interjected.

"Yes. I was about five, and he was a few years older than me when he died of a brain tumor."

"And I remember you somehow felt responsible for his death. How was that?"

"Yeah, that was because I didn't pray. See, when my brother was in the hospital, my family and some other people got together for kind of a prayer meeting . . . which was unusual for my family because we didn't normally do things like that. And they invited me to be part of it, but I said no. I went outside and played instead. Then, when my brother died, I was haunted by the feeling that it was my fault because I hadn't prayed for my brother. And all the good things I did in my life after that were a frantic effort to make up for what I'd done . . . I had to make everything right because I had done this terrible thing."

"But it was never enough," I added.

"Never. And there was no joy or peace in it. And the actual memory we prayed about was my memory of being at my brother's funeral. I felt so totally alone . . . like no one was there for me. I know there must have been adults around, but I don't remember anyone being there. And I had this very clear picture of myself walking alone back to the drinking fountain . . . and just sobbing. You helped me pray about that and visualize Jesus there with me, kneeling down and wrapping me in his arms. It didn't matter what I was thinking, *he was there!* Since there was no true guilt, there was no need of a word of forgiveness from him. He didn't do anything but to hold me. I can still picture that clearly now! And you know, just having that scene in my mind, it was like God let me know, 'This is a start . . . and we're going to face *everything together!*'"

"So that new way of looking at this experience has remained for you?"

"Oh, yes, it has! In fact, I use it a lot now when I'm frustrated or mad at myself. I visualize that little girl with Jesus. He was there for me then, and he's with me now. When I've hurt someone's feelings and feel guilty, I know he knows me and still cares for me. I feel God's love. And it opens me to care for others."

"Wow, that's great!" I exclaimed.

"Yeah. It actually gave me a pattern for how to deal with Pam's death," continued Jamie, referring to our mutual friend Pam who had recently died of cancer in her midthirties. "I kind of know what to do now. Bringing that memory to Jesus . . . it's made my relationship with God *grow.* I had always known it was *my* problem—not being able to trust God. But I couldn't figure out *why!* Now, I'm in a different place than I was—a totally different place. I honestly think it affects my life every day!"

"Jamie," I said, "I am so glad to hear what a blessing this whole experience has become for you."

"Me too! Believe me! Before God showed me all this, I kind of felt like I was in one of those games where you bop something and it pops up somewhere else."

"I know the kind," I said with a smile.

"I had read zillions of self-help books for self-esteem, when it was really a core belief! You know, when you start looking at core beliefs, you see things as they *are.* That's a difficult process too, but it's the right order to get real change—first the *root,* then the leaves."

"That's a really good way of putting it!" I replied.

"And in a strange way, I think God even used the thyroid problems I was having last year to help me face this thing. It slowed me down enough to hear God. Often, you can run from these things just by being busy!"

Myself: Guilt over an Accident

One winter, my older sister invited us to visit her and her husband at their cabin in northern Minnesota to go snowmobiling. My teenage daughter invited a friend (whose parents were also good friends of my wife and I) to come along on the outing. At one point during the afternoon, I was out on one snowmobile, and my daughter and her friend were with me on the other machine. The girls had asked me if they had to wear helmets, and I had said no, thinking we weren't going to be driving fast or going anywhere too dangerous. Things were going along fine until we were going through a wooded area. Suddenly, my daughter's sled caught one ski on a fallen log, and the sled was upended. My daughter's friend, Jenny, was sent flying through the air, and when she hit the ground, she struck her head on the end of a sawed-off log. She was knocked out cold!

I saw the event out of the corner of my eye and spun around to go back to them. When I got there, I saw that my daughter was fine, but Jenny was lying motionless in the snow with her face turned to one side and her eye staring blankly ahead. I thought she might be dead. And I was terrified!

I sent my daughter on my snowmobile to get help, and I stayed behind with Jenny, who I could now see was still breathing but unconscious. I spent about ten anxious minutes until help arrived. Slowly, Jenny came to, and we got her to a place where an ambulance could pick her up.

In the hospital, it was ascertained that Jenny had a skull fracture. As her brain began to swell, she lost consciousness again and was rushed by ambulance to a larger hospital for further treatment. The next days were a blur of waiting, hoping, and praying as the doctors did what they could to minimize the effects of Jenny's injury. I learned that brain trauma can take from six to twenty-four months to heal, and Jenny spent weeks in the hospital during that initial stretch of recovery.

About a week after the accident, my family and I were visiting Jenny in the hospital. Her parents gave me one of the most wonderful gifts I have ever received that day when they told me they forgave me for not making sure the girls had helmets on during our snowmobiling. This allayed one of my great fears—that this incident would ruin our deep and long-standing friendship. But now I was left to deal with my own feelings, and they were monstrous!

All that week, I had been kicking myself, thinking, "Why didn't I have us all wear helmets! Why!" The scene of Jenny's face lying unconscious in the snow haunted me like a specter day and night. And the guilt felt like a heavy weight on my shoulder.

Finally, I realized I needed to bring this traumatic memory to Jesus. So I got alone and cried out to God to deliver me from these haunting memories. As I prayed, asking Jesus to help me, the scene of Jenny's face in the snow came into my mind. Then something happened. Her eye, which had looked so lifeless, suddenly looked right at me and winked playfully! And somehow, I knew that Jesus was in that eye. Then the camera seemed to zoom out on my memory, and I saw myself kneeling over Jenny's body. But now Jesus was kneeling over *me*. Then my attention spread out even farther, and I saw all the leafless trees in the winter forest. They were filled with angels! The angels were singing and praising God!

What could all this mean! I asked God, "Are you trying to tell me something?"

Then as I sat quietly and thought about what I had seen, I realized that all three scenes corresponded to something that needed healing in my mind. First of all, I was concerned for Jenny. And when Jesus winked at me through Jenny's eye, it was like he was assuring me that he was *in Jenny* and would be helping her through the healing process. Secondly, when I saw Jesus kneeling over me, I came to realize that Jesus was helping me, even as I was trying to help Jenny. I had felt so alone and helpless, kneeling over her there in the forest. But Jesus let me see that I was *not* alone, that he had been with me. And as I thought about the scene with the angels all around us, I realized this tragic accident had introduced the subtle, despairing thought into my mind that the world is a place that is somehow out of control, where anything can happen. But seeing the angels in the forest assured me that God was still in control—he had everything in his hands.

I can only wonder what my life would have been like if Jesus had not released me from those chains of guilt and recrimination. How glad I am that he is still the God who sets the captives free!

Note: Jenny went on to make a wonderful recovery that surprised the doctors in several ways. And three years after the accident, Jenny's mother, still our good friend, told me that God had used that whole experience to work many blessings of character and growth into Jenny's life. Only God can take our tragedies and turn them into blessings!

80 03

Kyle: Witness to Suicide

Kyle was a young man of twenty-five with short brown hair and a trim beard. He held his lower jaw out slightly in a way that gave the impression of one trying hard to keep his emotions in. He told me how his father had been a workaholic as well as an alcoholic who sometimes beat his mother. When Kyle was twelve, his parents had divorced and decided he would live with his dad. He told me how his favorite cousin had died of acute respiratory infection that same year. He had also tasted death later in his youth when the girl next door, whom he had known since kindergarten, died in an auto accident.

"She was on her way to a babysitting job," Kyle reported, "when she ran a stop sign and got T-boned by another car. She was killed instantly. Oh yeah, then there was my best friend in high school who shot himself in the head with a shotgun. We were all pretty shocked by that one."

It didn't surprise me when, as our conversation moved on, Kyle said that death was his greatest fear as a child.

We talked on, and the topic turned to Kyle's beliefs about God.

"I grew up a Lutheran, but I kind of lost touch with God . . . so many bad things happening. Now I'm not sure *what* to believe!" admitted Kyle.

"Would you like a thought or two about that?" I offered.

"Yes, I would very much," said Kyle.

"Obviously, one of the big questions we have to face spiritually is death. Why does God allow it, since it violates everything we hold dear about life?"

Kyle nodded.

"Now the answer, according to the Bible," I continued "is that God doesn't want death to end our lives and has prepared a better place for us, which he has secured through the resurrection of Jesus. But not only does he need to make a better place, he also needs to make *us better.* Otherwise, we'd be like the dysfunctional family who moves into a new house and, in no time, has turned it into a dump heap. You could take 'em to *another* new home, and they'd do the same thing."

Kyle nodded again.

"So God not only needs to make us a better place, he needs to make us a better people."

"And it's up to us to change, right?" offered Kyle.

"Well, we're involved, but initially, the process of change starts with something *God* did," I said. "Kyle, just in our conversation so far, you've admitted to me that you've lied, hurt others, and used others for their money."

"That's right," Kyle admitted.

"And for those kind of things, we all deserve to be punished. But what I believe *God* did was to send his Son, Jesus, into the world. And the greatest gift Jesus gave us was dying for us. He took our punishment, paid our fine. And then he could truly say, 'Father, forgive them, they don't know what they're doing.' That was how he showed his love for us.

"But then there's the question of how does that get worked into our lives. And that's where our change comes in. The Bible calls it repentance. Jesus called people to 'repent and believe the Good News' that we're forgiven by his death. *Repent* actually means to 'change our mind.' So it's the process of changing our mind from trying to do things *our* way, which will only ruin us, to doing things his way. The twelve steps of recovery refer to it as 'praying for the knowledge of his will and the strength to carry it out.' Or as Jesus put it, 'Your will, not mine, be done.' Does that make sense?" I asked.

"Yes," replied Kyle. "That actually sheds light on this whole matter!"

"And I believe this is God's answer to death . . . which it seems you've experienced a lot of!"

"You can say that again!" agreed Kyle. "And there's also the time I saw a lady commit suicide. She stood in front of a train!

She was holding a sandbag and leaned forward, pointing her head right at the train."

"Oooh!" I said, feeling the shock of what Kyle told me. "Were you in a car when you saw this?"

"Yes, I had just pulled up to the railroad crossing, but there was no time to help her. One minute I saw her on the tracks, and the next, the train came by. It hit her full speed."

"So she was carried away by the train?"

"She actually kind of bounced off it. She flew through the air for about forty feet. Her head just exploded. And she looked like a helicopter—her arms and legs spread out. That happened five years ago when I was twenty, and I still see that scene every day in my mind!"

"Oh, Kyle!" I expressed. "Would you like to pray and ask Jesus to get into that experience for you and give you some comfort?"

"Yes, I would very much!"

"Would you like to pray or shall I?" I asked.

"Would you, please?"

"Certainly. Lord Jesus," I prayed, "please come and comfort Kyle and heal the wound he suffered when he saw this woman commit suicide. And, Lord, whatever drove her to that place of hopelessness and despair, I pray that she might, if possible, find rest in you. But in any case, would you help Kyle with his terrifying experience?"

I paused, still holding Kyle's hand, then said softly, "Kyle, having prayed about this, can you picture Jesus there with you in any way?"

"Actually, I was just doing that," Kyle replied.

"How do you see him?" I asked.

"He has his left hand on my shoulder."

"How does it feel to have him there?"

"Kind of serene. Definitely relief! Like things are going to be OK."

"Is that a good place to leave that memory?" I asked.

"Yes," said Kyle.

"Would you like to thank Jesus for his comfort?"

"Thank you, God," Kyle prayed softly. "That was amazing!" said Kyle, opening his eyes.

"Do you think that's going to help you with that memory in the future?" I asked.

"Oh, definitely!" stated Kyle.

ℰℭ

Helen: Sexual Assault

Helen had a bouncy manner that made her appear much younger than her thirty-seven years. Her bright smile seemed to have something of the energy and innocence of a young teenager in it. Her reddish-brown hair, pulled back in a ponytail, added even more youthfulness to her appearance. As she began to tell me her story, however, I soon saw that beneath her smile were some genuine hurts that had begun early and lasted long.

"I lived with my mother until she died of breast cancer when I was eleven," Helen began. "Then I went to live with my uncle and aunt. But my uncle was kind of abusive."

"Do you have some bad memories from those days?" I asked.

"Oh yeah! Both my uncle and aunt yelled at me a lot. My uncle tried to rape me a couple of times. The one time was when we were sleeping out in a fish house during the winter. But I fought him off and ran outside—I only had my boots and my nightgown. I remember I ran to the shore and stood there in the dark for a long time. Finally, he came and told me he wouldn't touch me, and I went back to the fish house. The other time was at a cabin up north. There were lots of people, but he and I were in a room with one bed. When he tried to mess around with me,

I fought him off again and ran outside. I remember being so mad and scared! I was shaking as I stood outside in the rain."

I could see that Helen had painful memories that needed God's healing, but we had only begun to talk, and I felt the need to listen a while longer. "Where was your father during your childhood years?" I asked.

"My mom and dad divorced when I was five. After that, we moved from Kansas City to Minnesota, and I really never saw him much after that. But my mom and older brother and sister and I were really close." A smile curled the edges of her lips as Helen reminisced, "Mom used to take us to a movie once a month, and afterwards, we would go to Walgreens drug store for banana splits. Then after Mom died, us kids were split up. My brother and sister went to a foster home up north, and I went to live with my uncle and aunt. I think they felt obligated to help, but they didn't figure they could take care of us all. So they took me because I was the youngest. I tried hard to please them. I kind of acted like a maid, doing a lot of cleaning and stuff. But it seemed whatever I did was not good enough for them. They had one daughter, three years older than I, and they treated us very differently. She got new clothes and lots of nice things, and I had to go to school in really old-fashioned clothes that my aunt picked up at used-clothing stores. It made school really hard. I got made fun of quite a bit. I remember feeling lonely a lot."

"I can see why," I responded. "You lost your dad at age five. Then your mom died at eleven. And then you were separated from the only people you still had that you loved—your brother and sister."

"You know, in a strange sort of way, it almost feels like what happened in my childhood was another life, totally separate from the one I'm living now."

"When did your *present* life begin?"

"When I graduated high school and moved up north to be near my brother and sister. But it was somehow never the same. I never made any close friends there, and I was never even able to get close to my family again after that. You know, I remember something inside me closing up after my uncle did that to me. It's like after that point, I never let people get close to me."

I began to feel a deep, aching sadness in my heart for this girl who had been betrayed. "I can see why you'd close up. Your uncle, the very person who was supposed to *take care of you* had turned on you and *attacked* you! What's the message in that? Don't trust anyone!"

"I guess that's about right." Helen went on telling me about her life, but I was having a hard time listening. The heartache I had begun to feel refused to go away but was instead getting stronger. I decided maybe it was God's way of telling me it was time for healing.

"I'm sorry to interrupt, Helen," I said, "but I'm having a hard time listening anymore. I just feel this deep sadness in my heart over the things that happened to you. Would you like to ask for God's help to heal some of these painful memories?"

"Yes, I would!" exclaimed Helen with a sigh of relief and eagerness.

"First of all, may I ask you what you believe about God?" I queried.

"Well, I never went to church or anything with my mom or uncle and aunt. But I did have a grandma—it was my aunt's mother, so she really wasn't any relation to me—and I used to spend two weeks with her during the summer. She was so kind to me, and she was a very spiritual woman. She took me to church and taught me all the prayers that I know. I always wanted what she had spiritually, but somehow, I was never able to make the connection with God myself. Then when I grew up and got married, I joined the Catholic Church. But . . ." Helen paused, searching for a way to express herself.

"But you were still searching for God more than finding him?"

"Yes! But it's odd, you know. Several times in my life, I have felt like I was just on the verge of getting to know God, but it never happened."

"Helen, could I tell you some of what I believe about God?"

"Yes, I wish you would! I actually spoke with Suzzie, who had talked with you a while back. And when I saw the difference it made in her life, I was eager to talk to you and see if you could help me get God's help with some of these things."

"Well, Helen, for me, it all goes back to the person of Jesus. I believe his claim that he was the Son of God—God came into this world as a man so that we could connect with him. The thing that I think is so marvelous about Jesus's life is that *he shared in our suffering.* The Bible says that on the cross, he bore the sin of the entire world. In other words, he felt the pain of your parent's divorce, the loss of your mother, the separation from your brother and sister, and the agony of having your uncle attack you! He suffered those things as part of his suffering on the cross, just so that he could be with you in those experiences. But the story goes on to tell how he rose from the dead, which to me says that his presence in our suffering can help us rise up from the deaths we've experienced. Helen, would you like to pray and ask Jesus to help you heal from these painful memories?"

"Yes, I would."

"I like to join hands when I pray. Is that OK with you?"

"Sure," said Helen, taking my hands as we bowed our heads. I could tell Helen was not used to praying aloud, but as she began, her words were simple and genuine. "Dear Jesus, I really want you to come into my life and help me heal from some of the things that have happened to me. I want you to help me be strong so I can take good care of my kids. Jesus, I just want you in my life."

"Helen," I said looking up and into her eyes. "I sometimes find great help from just picturing Jesus there with me in my most troubling times. It seems to me that what happened to you with your uncle made a deep impact on you and, like you said, kind of closed you up emotionally. When you described those memories to me, both of them ended with you standing out in the dark, cold and alone. Would you like to ask Jesus to meet you there in those memories?"

"Yes! Dear Jesus," Helen went right on, "I'm so tired of this hurt! I don't want to be in the darkness anymore. Please come to me and help me!"

Both Helen and I had begun to cry now. I had almost no doubts as I asked Helen, "Can you see Jesus coming to you?"

Helen paused for a moment and then said, "Yes, I can."

"How does he look?" I asked.

"He's like a bright light, and his arms are reaching out to me!"

"Can you see yourself going to him and letting him take you in his arms?"

"Oh yes!" The tears were coming in earnest now. "He's so warm!"

I wrapped my arms around Helen and hugged her tightly as she cried tears of joy. "I think Jesus wants to tell you," I said, "that he's been waiting so eagerly for this moment."

After a short while, we sat back in our chair and reached for tissues to dry our eyes. Both of us were just about giddy with joy over what Jesus had done for Helen and spoke our praise of him to each other.

"Is there any more you feel you need to talk about today?" I asked after a few moments.

"No," Helen beamed a radiant smile, "this is what I needed!"

We talked for some time more about how Helen could deepen her relationship with Jesus by reading his Word and meeting with other believers in fellowship.

After we had finished, Helen reflected, "You know, I think it's neat that you don't, like, pretend to have all the answers. You just pointed me to Jesus, and you were as amazed as me at what he did!"

How true.

Ruthie: Childhood Sexual Abuse

Ruthie was a tall young woman in her late twenties with short blond hair. She entered my office and sat down to go through her fifth step of treatment for alcoholism. She began to tell me the contours of her life story: parents divorced when she was two, raised by her mom thereafter, made several moves in her youth until she finally settled into a small city in Minnesota. When we got to the subject of abuse, she mentioned that she had been molested by several of her older cousins between the ages of eight and twelve.

"How did those experiences make you feel?" I asked.

"Scared! I was always scared every time it would happen. But after a while, I began to wonder if that was just the way life was—if this was somehow normal."

"So it was confusing too?" I offered.

"Yes."

Ruthie went on to describe how hard it is to face those cousins when she sees them today.

"I have actually never told anybody about this before. I sure would like to get this taken care of somehow. But I really don't know how," admitted Ruthie.

I sat up in my chair and replied, "Would you like some ideas on that?"

"Sure!" exclaimed Ruthie.

"As I have listened and worked with people as they heal from experiences like that, I have observed three steps that people go through," I began. "The first is to tell the story. The second is to identify the feelings and effects this experience had on you. The third is to take a spiritual step of healing and forgiveness, which seems to require God's help. Does that make sense?"

"Yes, it does."

"Would you like to work on this a little bit?" I offered.

"Yes, I would," replied Ruthie.

"OK, the first step—tell the story. An experience like this one leaves us with a lot of shame because what was done to you was very wrong. It wasn't *your* wrong, but it can leave you carrying a load of shame. The first step in breaking that shame is simply to bring into the light what happened—to tell the story of what took place in such a way that *your* heart is satisfied."

"So you want me to, like, tell you what actually happened?" Ruthie queried.

"I don't want you to do anything," I clarified. "But if *you* want to tell the story, in whatever depth you would like to, I will be glad to listen. Would you like to tell your story?"

"Yes, I would," Ruthie said with a smile of understanding.

"Well, I remember when my cousin James used to babysit me," Ruthie began. She recounted five or six episodes that were vivid in her memory.

When she finished, I responded, "Good. Now how about if we tackle the second step—identifying effects. You've already explained some of the feelings this experience left you with. What were they . . . scared and confused?"

"That's right."

"Were there any others?"

"I felt dirty, somehow. Violated. Like something had been taken away from me."

"And what was it that was taken from you? A sense of safety?"

"Yes. And my own sense of wholeness, somehow."

"What about your relationships with other people? Have you noticed any ways that this experience affected the way you relate to others?"

"Oh yeah! It's made it really hard for me to have a sexual relationship with a man. As soon as they get close to me or touch me . . ." Ruthie trailed off.

"All that old fear comes back to you?" I questioned.

"Yep."

"Anything else? Any other feelings or effects?"

"Not that I can think of," replied Ruthie.

"OK, how about if we go on to step three—taking a step of healing and forgiveness?"

"OK."

"The goal here is to be able to let go of this experience so that bitterness over what took place doesn't eat *you* up. Do you know what I mean?"

"Yes, I do," said Ruthie with a knowing nod.

"And this is where I find it helpful to look to God. I actually rely on Jesus, who I believe was the Son of God, because of his amazing ability to forgive."

Ruthie nodded.

"And actually, Ruthie, there's one more reason I depend on Jesus. He died on the cross, carrying the sins of the whole world on his back. But then he rose back to life. And to me, that says that he has the ability to help us rise back to life after some of the things that have happened to us. Would you say that, in some way, something inside you died as a result of this experience?"

"Yes, I would," admitted Ruthie.

"And wouldn't it be nice if Jesus could get into that situation and bring that part of you back to life?!"

"Oh yeah!"

"Ruthie, would you like to forgive those cousins for what they did to you?"

"Yes, I would. I really would," replied Ruthie, a little amazed at her own answer.

"You see, now, why we went through steps 1 and 2 first? Because when you forgive these guys, you're not just forgiving them for what took place on a few nights long ago. You're forgiving them for all the suffering you've experienced as a result of what they did. Those experiences have hurt you for years. And *that's* what you're forgiving. Ruthie," I said gingerly, "would you like to pray right now and tell God you forgive those guys?"

"Yes," said Ruthie.

We joined hands, and Ruthie began. "Lord, thank you that I've had a chance to talk about this thing today with Pastor Mark. I forgive John and Sam and Jerry for what they did to me. I want to leave it behind me. And I pray that you would help them get over this too, 'cause I'm sure it probably affected them too. In Jesus's name, amen."

We raised our heads and looked into each other's eyes. "How did that feel?" I asked.

"Good. It felt good. It really felt like something inside changed. Kind of like something was lifted off me. It's good!" stated Ruthie with a chuckle.

"I'm glad," I affirmed. "Ruthie, I believe there is actually one more thing to attend to and that's healing *you*. It's kind of a part B in the step 3 of spiritual healing. It's really a prayer that God would help you overcome all the negative effects of this experience. That he would heal the inner wounds and bring back to life the things that were lost or died in you as a result of this wrong. You did a marvelous job of extending forgiveness. And you can see how important that is to do because until you forgive, you're wrapped up in bitterness." I bared my teeth and growled like a mad dog. Ruthie laughed. "And it's not really possible to pray for healing when we're all caught up in bitterness. But now that you've taken that step to forgive, you're free to ask God to help *you* heal. Would you like to pray again, Ruthie, and ask God for that?"

"Yes I would. Lord Jesus," Ruthie prayed, "would you help me to heal from the effects of what happened when I was a girl? I think I really need you to help me overcome this stuff so it's not controlling me anymore."

Ruthie paused and I quietly asked her, "Ruthie, can you picture Jesus there with you in those memories of what happened?"

"Yes, I can."

"How do you see him?"

"He's walking with me."

"How does it feel to have him there?"

"Good. Peaceful. Like everything's going to be OK. Like he's going to help me get over this stuff."

"And when you see those memories now, do you feel OK?"

"Yeah. Because *he's* there now!"

"Is that a good place to leave things?" I asked.

"Yes," stated Ruthie, opening her eyes and smiling at me.

"Wow!" Ruthie exclaimed, "That was neat. It's like I was looking down from above and I could see him walking with me!"

"When you say 'him,' you mean . . ."

"Jesus," replied Ruthie meekly. "Before, when I prayed to forgive those guys, it felt really good. But this was different. It felt really good but in a different way. Like this took care of another part of my need."

"You feel this was what you needed, then?" I asked.

"Exactly!"

Looking upward, I said, "Thank you, Lord."

Ruthie looked up and nodded.

From Here

Well, that's about it. Not that I couldn't fill more pages with stories of people like Bobby who walked in on his best friend who had committed suicide and "time stopped." Or Rob whose first girlfriend was shot and killed in a hunting accident, and he's been "running from God ever since." Or Homer who had to make the decision to pull the plug on his mother after she had a brain aneurism and had been tormented with second-guessing ever since. And I could tell you how Jesus met each of these people and brought peace into the nightmares in their minds.

But you've probably pretty much got the idea by now of what Jesus can do. The question now is, what will *we* do?

As you've been reading these pages, perhaps something from your past has come back to your mind. Maybe it's something you're *convinced* you had put behind you. (Or you're letting 'sleeping dogs lie' or you weren't going to 'dig up old garbage' or some other saying that we hear that only keeps the poison buried in our souls!) And yet it keeps resurfacing in your mind.

If that's the case, may I ask you, is God a part of that picture? If not, if you're struggling to carry that painful memory alone, maybe you would like to ask Jesus to help you see him there.

It may be that you could use some help with this memory—somebody to listen to you as you tell the story. Don't hesitate to call a trusted friend, pastor, or family member. Remember, telling the story is the first step to healing. Then you can identify the effects of the event and pray for healing (and forgiveness, if needed).

Taking It to Others

As we experience the presence of Jesus in our painful memories, and as we find our souls "stilled and quieted . . . like a weaned child with its mother" (Psalm 131:2), it's only natural to want to share the blessing with others.

A good place to start may be with prayer: Lord, may *your will* (that people are healed from the wounds of their past) be done here in *my* circle of friends as it is done in heaven. Then keep your eyes peeled for the open doors God will set before you.

A friend of mine recently pulled me aside and admitted he was struggling inwardly with discouragement and apathy. He asked if I had any suggestions for him. I said no but offered to pray and ask God to show him what could be causing his bad feelings. He accepted my offer to pray (although he was, at the time, an agnostic), and so I asked God to help my friend and show him what could be at the root of his problems. After our prayer, we talked on, and within minutes, my friend began telling me about how, when he was eighteen, his older brother had committed suicide. His response to the situation was to turn his back on God (since he couldn't bear the thought of his brother burning in hell forever). That discussion with my friend has opened up an ongoing dialogue in which we are looking at the scriptures together for answers about God, death, and the saving work of Jesus. Eventually, I pray that my friend can be healed from the wounds of his past and the lies that have crippled his spirit.

I wonder what doors God will open for you in the lives of the people you know. I wonder what will happen as you ask them questions like, "Do you want to tell me about it?" "What do you believe about God . . . Jesus?" "Would you like to pray with me about that?" and "Can you picture Jesus there with you in that scene?"

If you end up in the middle of some God-glorifying stories that you would like to share with me, don't hesitate to drop me a note on Facebook at Mark I. Peske. Or maybe I'll run into you and hear some of your stories in heaven, where *all* our wounds will be healed, where we'll see Jesus face-to-face, and where *all* our nightmares will finally and fully be turned to the sweetest of dreams.

Till then, peace be with you!